Love Music

Hate Cancer

How the Blues,
Bohemian Rhapsody
& Chemotherapy
Saved My Life

A Survivor's Story

by

Mark Telesca

Foreword by

Dr. Janice Johnston, MD

Jenifer Skolnick, Editor

Copyright © 2020 Mark Telesca

All rights reserved. No part of this book may be reproduced or transmitted in any form or by any means without written permission from the author.

ISBN-13: 9781655695094

*"I feel like I'm here for a reason.
I feel like I'm here to accomplish something.
I still don't know exactly what that is.
I can't pinpoint the reason for my existence.
But I know I'm on the right path."*

- Mark Telesca

LOVE MUSIC
HATE CANCER

DEDICATION

This book is dedicated to anyone who is going through cancer or any other health issues. This kind of struggle happens to so many of us, so it's important for us to share our stories.

This way we know – we are not alone.

LOVE MUSIC HATE CANCER

CONTENTS

	Foreword	ix
	Preface	xi
1	Everybody Has A Story	1
2	What's Goin' on?	11
3	Chemotherapy & Other Stuff	25
4	The Blues	36
5	Bohemian Rhapsody	44
6	The Funky Biscuit	53
7	Cancer Can Rock	65
8	Let's Get Real	85
9	Now What?	100
	Epilogue	107
	Appendix	109
	Thank You	115
	Share Your Story	116
	An Exercise in Visualization	127

FOREWORD

A compelling account of just how hearing those three words "you have cancer" can affect every aspect of your life, relationships, and outlook on life.

As a physician, I have to be the bearer of this news on a too frequent basis. Any cancer diagnosis is overwhelming. Patients want to know, will I die, how long will I live, how sick will I get with treatment, will I be able to work? The question that comes up most often, unfortunately, is how will I pay for this? That's the last thing one wants to worry about when you're fighting for your life. Even with insurance, the co-pays and deductibles can be too much for any individual.

Mark details just how cancer affected every aspect of his life and how he dealt with overcoming his potentially devastating disease.

Beating cancer isn't all about the chemotherapy, surgery, or radiation. Making sure you have the support emotionally from family and friends can make all the difference getting through day by day.

I had the honor of helping in a small way with Mark's recovery through a program offered by the Blues Foundation. The Blues Foundation's HART Fund helps blues musicians with medical and dental expenses, and funeral expenses, in addition to offering free preventative health screenings throughout the year. The program supports so many blues musicians and helps to keep them making America's truest art form, the blues, alive and well.

Mark's story is real and will be helpful to anyone going through treatment and recovery from cancer. I, for one, am so eternally grateful that this bad ass bass player is around to tell it.

Dr. Janice Johnston, MD
Chair, The Blues Foundation's HART Fund
Medical Director, Redirect Health

PREFACE

My name is Mark. I was born in Brooklyn, New York in the winter of 1961. I'm a husband, a dad, a son, a brother, and an uncle. I guess you could say I'm a family man. I am also a bass player, a singer, a songwriter, a guitar player and band leader. I'm a college graduate and I am a licensed funeral director in two states and I'm a guy who loves the blues.

I am a cancer survivor.

I'm the guy who gets up every morning and makes the coffee and walks the dogs. I'm just a regular working guy with one exception. My job is to go out to a different bar almost every night of the week where I play and sing the blues. Most regular guys don't do that. There are a few, but not too many.

I'm not going to bore you with too many specific details about my life, but I am going to give you an overview of who I am and where I came from and what makes me tick.

I will share the things I have learned while going through chemotherapy treatments. I am going to let you know what my life is like now, after successfully beating cancer. I am going to connect you with some of the groups and organizations that have helped me along the way. I will tell you what I did in my own personal fight against this disease. This book is about the things that I did – that I truly believe helped me become a survivor – and how life is different for me today.

I hope this book helps you, or a beloved relative or friend, find the strength you will need when and where you need it. I hope that you find this book to be informative, uplifting and inspirational. I hope it helps you believe that there are better days ahead.

LOVE MUSIC HATE CANCER

1

EVERYBODY HAS A STORY

This is mine…

As I lie here in my hospital bed in the recovery room at Bethesda Memorial Hospital East, in Boynton Beach, Florida, I can't help but think about the beautiful new home my wife, Karene, and I just built and moved into 30 days ago with our two chihuahuas, Bailee and Lola.

I'm on the verge of tears – again. I can't believe the three words I just heard. I knew in a second that my life had just changed forever.

My surgeon, Dr. Faresi walks in, sits at my bedside, takes my hand, and says, "You have cancer." After a long pause, he then says, "I'm sorry." I am speechless. I am devastated.

I somehow find the strength to call Karene and tell her the news. She is at the hospital within minutes. We wait for further instruction from the medical staff. A small, unassuming man in a white coat enters my room. He is obviously another doctor. He looks at his paperwork and checks the room number on the door. He looks at me and says, "Are you Mark?" "Yes." With that, he gets down on one knee, he also takes my hand, and says, "Don't worry too much about it. You're going to be fine." He is smiling and he is radiant. He is confident, and for some reason I know he is telling the truth.

I don't know how or why I know this; I just know it. He gently puts my wife and myself at ease. I instantly know that this doctor, who is barely five feet tall, is going to be a giant in my life.

With all the positive feelings and encouragement I had initially received from the doctors and the medical staff, I was still obviously very devastated over this news.

I began a new life in an instant. My new life was very scary for me. Everything was going to change, and I knew it. I immediately started thinking of my own mortality and the realization of actually dying was in the forefront of all my thoughts. In an instant I started thinking back into my past, way back to when I was a young child. I hadn't done that for decades. I was remembering all sorts of events that I had thought I had forgotten.

I was only three or four years old and I remember living in South Ozone Park in Queens, NY.

That's where my mom's family was. All my aunts and uncles and cousins were right there in the neighborhood. My family lived in a two-story apartment building. I lived there with my mom, my dad, and my older sister Donna.

Those were good days. My sister and I shared a bedroom and we would play together when we were home. She's awesome. We would just let our imaginations run wild. We didn't have too many toys, but we had some. She had her dolls and I had a bag of those green plastic army men. I used to dig the army guys as a kid. GI Joe and all that stuff. My sister and I would drive around the world sitting on the edge of the bed. My mother would let us use an old pot cover. That was the steering wheel. That's how we got around. I would always be the driver; I still am. Whenever I go somewhere with my wife these days, I am always the driver. I don't know why, that's just the way it is.

I remember the simple things from my youth. I think we all do. I remember my mother sitting by the second-story window of that old apartment house on 128th Street. She would be hanging the clothes on the clothesline to dry, and every once in a while, the line would get stuck and somebody's shirt – or, God forbid, someone's pair of underwear – would be hanging on the line for the whole day and for the whole neighborhood to see.

We lived right by John F. Kennedy Airport. I remember looking out my bedroom window watching the airplanes fly over. I never gave it a second thought; it was just regular life for me. They would come in so low, and so loud, and so often that after a while you didn't even hear them or notice them anymore.

I did all the things that kids did in those days. I would get up every morning and walk my sister to school with my mom. School was right down the block across the street and on the next corner. It was a Catholic school attached to St. Anthony's Roman Catholic Church, and it was tough. The teachers and the nuns were allowed to hit the kids. One of my cousins ended up getting a concussion from one of the nuns who hit her on the head with a stack of books! This was in the early 1960s. Nothing was done about it. There was not even any reprimand for this nun. I do remember the family being very upset. If anything like that happened today, she would lose her job and the school would be sued. But, it was a different time. It was a simpler time, and I liked it.

I too attended kindergarten at St. Anthony's Roman Catholic Church, the same school my sister went to for kindergarten. The year was 1966 or maybe 1967. It doesn't really matter now. That was the year when we packed up all of our stuff and moved all the way out to Long Island. You see, in Queens, I had aunts, uncles, cousins, everybody, and they really loved me, and I really loved them. So, when we moved out to Long Island, it was all over. There was no one left. It was just me and my father and my mother and my sister.

We were approaching the mid-late 1960s, sort of the end of the baby boom. There were lots and lots of kids around. All my neighbors had three or four kids. Some had five. One family who lived around the corner had 13 children. They were a big, big family, and they were very Catholic. Growing up, everyone in my neighborhood was either Irish or Italian, but everybody was white, and everybody was Catholic.

It was just the neighborhood I lived in. We rode our bikes, we played army in the street hiding in all the neighbors' shrubs. We would use twigs and branches as pretend guns and shoot and kill each other. We would all fight about it. I shot you, you're dead! I'm not dead! You are so dead! You didn't shoot me, you missed, I shot you so you're dead! We could never agree on who was actually dead or alive. It's unimportant now, but I do remember we all had a real good time hanging out together.

We played every sport imaginable, right in the middle of the street. We did everything together, all the kids on the block. The girls, the boys, it didn't matter. It was kind of nice. I spent a lot more time with the kids in the street than I did with my own family.

My father worked a lot. He would commute to his job in New York City by train. He would come home every day at the same time. Dinner was at 6:15 every day. Each night after dinner he would proceed to work on the house. He was kind of a handyman, much handier than I am. He liked to put up paneling. He paneled everything. Our whole house was paneled; everybody's house was paneled. The living room, the bedroom, the kitchen, all had paneling. Even the basement had paneling. He even put up some paneling in the garage and the shed. He went paneling crazy. Everyone did, it was just the thing to do. It was the

1970s man! I look back on that now and I just have to laugh.

I used to try to help around the house, but I really wasn't into it. Ok, the truth is, I was forced to help. I never liked physical labor. It just wasn't my thing. It still isn't my thing. After a certain age of like 11 or 12 it was my job to mow the lawn. I used to hate mowing the lawn. I used to hate raking the leaves. I used to hate trimming the bushes. I still do. My parents used to yell at me all the time when it came time to do gardening or anything like that. They used to say, "You'd better never buy a house because you don't like to work." I have since bought two houses.

The truth is, I actually love to work, but I love to work at what I love to do. I'll work 24/7 if I feel it is worthwhile. You see, for me, I'd have rather stayed in Queens, where everything was concrete, so we could spend our time doing things we liked instead of spending our time fixing up an old house, and making sure the lawn looked good, and all the shrubs were just right.

Let's not forget about the car. We were out in Long Island now, so of course we needed a car. I don't remember us having a car before. Never really needed one but dad was commuting to the city every day now, so we had to have a car. Mom would drop him off at the railroad station and then she used the car all day bringing us kids to school and all that normal back and forth suburban action. She would then pick our dad up at the railroad station every evening. On the weekends, it was my dad's car. I remember him washing that car, and washing that car, and washing that car. Yeah, he liked his car to look good. These days I'm kind of the same way when it comes to my car, but I wasn't always like that. My brother-in-law is kind of obsessive about washing his cars too. Maybe there is something in the Long Island water.

I remembered my first day of first grade. Parkway Oaks, and my teacher was Mrs. Good. This was great. It can't get any better than that. Mrs. Good is my teacher, so what could possibly go wrong? Mrs. Good was okay.

First grade, second grade, third grade, I really liked all my teachers, and I kind of liked school at that time as well. I was never a great student. In fact, I was probably a little below average. I really had to work hard for good grades. And I never really wanted to work that hard for good grades. It just didn't seem that important to me at the time. You see, my sister, she got all the brains in the family. She had more brains than me, my mother and my father put together. She was a rock star when it came to getting good grades. It just came easily to her, but she did put in the work as well. She really liked academia.

Her good grades sort of made me feel bad. My folks used to say, "Why can't you be more like your sister?" I just wasn't into it. I wanted to do other things. I wanted to play baseball at this point in my life. That's what I really wanted to do. I just wanted to go out and play. I still do!

Music wasn't really a part of my life until I hit the

fourth grade. One day at school there was this big assembly. That was the day when all the students went into either band or orchestra, and all the kids were given an instrument. Each kid had a choice. This was a very big day for me. This is actually the first decision I am going to make for myself. I am pumped! You see, all my decisions were made for me up to this point. What to eat, what to wear, what time to do this, what time we are going to do that. Everything has been decided for me since day one.

I look at all the instruments. I have never seen anything like this before. After I got home, I told my folks about school that day. I was so excited to tell my parents that I chose to play the cello. I was told that I was not allowed to play the cello, that I was not allowed to play the bass, and that I was not allowed to be in the Orchestra. I was to play the trumpet like my Uncle Joe. My dad was serious; I was crushed.

I had an uncle who was a trumpet player. He was a good trumpet player and a good musician. He would always practice. He practiced until the day he died. I figure I'm going to do the same. He was my dad's brother, and this is how he made extra money. He made more money than my father did, and this is what was planned for me. The plan for me was to get some kind of city job when I grew up and play trumpet on the weekends in a wedding band. Just like my Uncle Joe. That was going to be my life. It was already planned out, and I was just a kid! Crazy, huh?

But there was a problem. I didn't want to play the trumpet, not to mention carrying it back and forth to school every day. That was a drag and I got picked on for it. Then there was the marching band. I hated marching band. I hated the uniforms I had to wear. I wanted to play in the orchestra with the wooden instruments. The orchestra would rehearse on the stage in the school auditorium. There was beautifully planked wood underneath the stage lights. As far as the school concert band goes, well, we were in some cold room, with a bunch of kids who didn't know how to play, blowing their brains out. It gave me such a headache to play the trumpet. I really didn't enjoy it.

But being a good son (and I was still trying to be a good boy at this point in my life), I played it because I didn't want to let my parents down. I just didn't want to do that. So, I played trumpet all the way up into high school, begrudgingly. I had some fun with it from time to time, but the orchestra was really my scene. That was what I wanted to do. In fact, when the orchestra would rehearse, I would stand in the back of the auditorium and listen to them playing classical music and I knew that was where I needed to be. It just never happened. I couldn't persuade my folks to allow me to make that switch. This was a turning point in my life. As I look back on it now, I think, that was the point when I really missed my destiny.

Destiny, now there's a word for you. Are we all destined to do something? Are we all destined to become something? I don't know. When I was in my 30's, that's what the fortune teller told me when I sat down, and she read my palm. She said, "You missed your destiny." I only went to the fortune teller that one time in my life when I was an adult.

By the time I was in middle school I started to feel a little resentful, all my decisions were still being made for me, and I wasn't allowed to make any decisions on my own, but enough about that for now. That's not what this book is about. I just wanted to give you a little idea of who I am and where I come from.

Let's go to my high school years. I'm lost, I don't know what to do, and I find myself joining this church folk group. Everybody would strum their guitars, and we would sing everything from "Kumbaya" to folk songs and maybe some Neil Young covers or songs like the Allman Brothers' "Ramblin' Man." We played whatever was popular on the radio in those days. The folk group would rehearse on Wednesday nights, and then play a 9:30 a.m. mass on Sundays. After mass, we would all go to McDonald's. It really was more of a social thing than anything else.

I'm not a very religious person. I wasn't religious then, and I'm even less religious now. I get religion; I think I understand it to some degree. I've read the Bible twice in my life and that's the truth. It's just about the only book I ever read cover to cover. You see, I think religion and organized church is very cool for some people. It creates a sense of community. A common thread that all who are in attendance share. But it's just not for me. My community, my church, is the blues.

2

WHAT'S GOIN' ON?

Things weren't going well for me in high school, and my grades certainly were suffering big time. I was really starting to feel lost. I had dropped out of the high school concert band by my senior year. I didn't have too many friends. I knew a lot of people, but not many of them I could call friends. I knew all the kids on my block, but some of them were a little older and they were going off to college and getting jobs after school. Things were changing!

I was content with the way things were. I was just sort of coming and going as I pleased, not really caring much about anything. I stopped caring about my grades. I stopped caring about my appearance. I stopped caring about being broke. I took on zero responsibility at this point in my life. I pretty much decided to stop caring about life. This of course was not one of the smarter decisions I have ever made.

I remember one day near the end of 12th grade. I remember this like it was yesterday. It was a perfect sunny day. It was the beginning of June. All my classmates were ready to get out of school and start their adult lives. That's all everyone was talking about. Then one of the teachers came in the room and passed out a pamphlet. Each student was required to fill out this form before graduation. I take mine and I slowly open it. On the pamphlet were my options.

Option #1: Are you going to go to college and continue your education? What school are you going to go to? What's your major going to be? Blah, blah, blah, all that stuff.

Option #2: Are you going to join the work force? What profession or trade are you going to be working in? Will you be remaining in the state?

Option #3: Which branch of the military are you going to be joining? Are you going into the reserves?

Option #4: Well, there was no option #4. And that's the one I chose. That's the one I had to choose. I never did fill out that form. You see, I had no idea what I was going to do.

Just like that, there was a moment of clarity. I could see things as they really were. Holy cow, what's going to happen next month after graduation? I have no plan, all kinds of thoughts like that. This was not going over well in my house. At this point in my life, my father really started berating me over my lack of direction, and not putting enough effort into things. I pretty much had zero options. I didn't have a job, so I couldn't move out, since I had no money. Things were not good.

You know, we all have to go through some tough times to really appreciate the good times. We are supposed to learn from our mistakes. It seems like I made just about every mistake you could possibly make. Eventually things started to come together, but that was much later in life.

I was starting to feel inferior. This is a very unhealthy way to feel and can lead to depression. Depression can be debilitating. I've seen it take down some very talented and extraordinary people. I believe that several factors can lead to depression.

I think I was a teenager with teenage depression. I will never really know for sure. We didn't get diagnosed for things like depression back then. You were either normal or crazy. Some of the signs of teenage depression are feeling sad most of the time, feeling hopeless, feeling like you want to give up on things. Not to mention, feeling worthless and riddled with excessive guilt.

I wasn't even really playing guitar yet. I had an acoustic guitar, and I used to strum it in that church folk group. That's where I really got my musical start. And I really dug playing the guitar. It really spoke to me. Acoustic guitar, I was never really much into electric guitar.

So, I thought that maybe I'd just play in some cafés. There were a lot of them around back then. They were in New York City, they were out in Long Island, and people seemed to be interested in that scene. I mean, there were great songs on the radio back then. The music landscape was changing. We were just getting out of the folk era, but there were still a lot of people interested in acoustic music. It wasn't like it is today.

Sometimes I feel like I'm a novelty. People walk into the restaurant with their kids, and it's like, "Oh, look at the guy wearing the pork pie hat, playing the guitar, and singing the blues."

I do some gigs where I feel more like a prop than anything else, but that's what it is like now, so let's get back to then.

So, I was strumming on guitar, figuring I'd be a guitar player. I decided that's what I was going to do. It wasn't easy telling my parents that because they thought it wasn't going to happen.

They were just not going to allow this to happen. My mother and father would ask my relatives to try to talk me out of playing music! I had zero support from my family on this and now times were getting tough for me. You see, I'd decided that this was really what I wanted to do, but I'm being forced to do something else.

All my life I was told by my parents, my friends' parents, my teachers, the clergy, aunts and uncles, my older cousins, and just about any adult I would have come in contact with, "You got to have something to fall back on." That was all I ever heard. I was the only one in my family interested in music enough to make it a full-time career and I could not have been more discouraged from doing so. So, guess what I did? That's right, I fell back in line. Just like everyone wanted me to do. I truly believe that they all did have my best interest in mind. I grew up in a world surrounded by people who really believed the only way to be successful was to conform. My folks hated the hippie thing; guys with long hair playing rock music was for losers. At least that was the way I was made to feel.

I remember getting a job delivering furniture. A couple of the older kids in the neighborhood bought furniture trucks and were delivering furniture for a living. I couldn't even imagine doing that now at this age! We were getting hired for $50 a day, or whatever it was we got for being out all-day delivering furniture. All summer long, and it sucked.

I was living at home and miserable. I'd drive to this miserable job in a broken-down car. I would work all day at a miserable job that sucked. I would come home to my parents' house and that sucked. Everything sucked and I was miserable.

I was still part of that folk group. I was strumming guitar at Sunday morning mass. It was fun. Nobody really gave a shit about your musicianship. It was just a hang, with some really nice people. They eventually set up the "Our Lady of Lourdes Folk Group" Facebook page. All of these years later, I'm still in contact with everyone, and I even see them occasionally, too. How crazy is that? This world we live in has seen so much change it's unbelievable and yet somehow the past is still with us.

At this point in my life, I wanted to switch gears and get myself into a local rock band. Everybody had an electric guitar, so I figured the easiest way to get involved in this scene was to play the bass. I hooked up with these neighborhood guys. We formed a band, and we sucked. I mean we really, really sucked. None of us knew how to play and we knew nothing about music but that was not going to stop us. We were getting looks from some girls and that was it! Ha! We were just trying to be cool.

We rented the basement of a beauty shop in a neighboring town for $100 a month. We'd go down there, and we could leave the drums and the PA system set up. It was kind of cool. We did a lot of hanging out there. A lot of hanging out. Like, every day when I wasn't working, and every single night of the week.

The drinking age was 18 at the time, so I was old enough to get into the bars, but I looked like I was 12 years old when I was 18. I was kind of uncomfortable in bars because everybody seemed to be older and hooked up. I just felt more like a recluse, still trying to figure out who I was at this point in my life.

All I could focus on was, "Why do I feel so out of

place?" As I look back now, I feel like the truth is that I was not getting anything done. Nothing was working out. This went on for a very long time.

I mean nothing was going on at all. I had no skills at all, but there were a lot of kids like that back then. You could get a manual labor job just about anywhere. It's not like it is today. It seems like almost every kid goes to college today. Many of them are getting an excellent education; however, there are so many unemployed college graduates, the numbers are staggering.

Everything back in the late 1970s and early 1980s was simpler, and I still couldn't keep it together! I had it good and I didn't even know how good I had it. My food was cooked and served to me, my clothes were clean, my bed was made for me (up to a certain age). If I could have just been able to handle the negativity and guilt that was always so present in that house, it would have been cool. But there was no chance of that ever happening.

Finally, when I was in my mid 20's I hooked up with these guys from Queens, NY. We got these gigs traveling to Puerto Rico and St. Thomas where we would just crash in a band house. We would get these 6 or 7 week-long gigs in restaurants that would turn into night clubs after dinner. We played all kinds of cover music. Then after the gig, we would party all night long and we would sleep all day. It was kind of a rock star thing for me back then. Live music was king, and we were the band coming in from New York City and it was really exciting. Especially when we first started out. But, after about 5 years of that it got old, real fast, and I was pushing thirty.

Thirty, now that is a big number and it was only a year or two away. If I didn't have my shit together by the time I was thirty, I figured the rest of my life would just suck. The band wasn't really getting along that well anymore and we were all getting a little tired of it. Truthfully, it became more about the partying, and less and less about the music with each passing year. We still keep in touch with each other and all we can do now is laugh about those days.

So, I quit the band and got a job in New York City that didn't work out, I had an apartment that didn't work out, got another job and another and they all didn't work out. Holy shit, I thought, "What am I going to do?" So, I went to college. I moved back in with my parents, put my tail between my legs, and I got serious about college. Very serious, I was in the Mortuary Science Program and I was on track to becoming a funeral director. I had a cousin who was in the funeral business and he was doing much better than me at the time. I got a job working at some local funeral homes for gas money. I was a pallbearer, and I would work nighttime services, go to cemeteries, drive limos, drive hearses, and I would even help pick up bodies for the funeral home. I also played in a local band on Friday and Saturday nights.

I was busy, and all I could focus on was the last place I wanted to be was at home with my parents at 30 years old! That, to me, would be a disgrace!

Here is a quick college story. I am two semesters away from graduating and I have this embalming class. This is a two-semester course. You cannot take the second semester until you successfully finish the first semester. The class is ridiculously difficult. It's all about chemicals and how to make embalming fluids and parts per millions and all kinds of technical stuff. I am starting to get burnt out on school and I am having a bit of trouble concentrating on all this stuff. There are three tests to take and a final. My first test comes, and I get something like a 42%. Second test, more like 56%. Better, but I am getting myself into serious trouble. If I fail this course, it is not offered again until the fall semester. Before the third test is given, I just happen to have some free plane tickets to Vegas with some friends. I know that I should not go to Vegas. But, I was convinced by some knuckleheads that it's all going to work out. "Don't worry about it!" they all said. "You'll be fine!" "Don't be a pussy!" So, I went to Vegas. Now, everyone knows I can't tell you what happened in Vegas, but I can tell you this. I got home late on a Sunday night. I walked into class on Monday morning right into test Number 3! Oh, I failed the test miserably. A few days later I went to the Dean of the Department and asked him if there was anything I could do. He said to me, "What happened to you? You were doing so well and it all just fell apart." At that moment I felt extremely embarrassed and I felt like I was letting down not only myself, but others as well. Then the Dean took out his Texas Instruments calculator and plugged it into the wall (this was almost 30 years ago). He went to the file cabinet and pulled out my grades for this class. He started pushing all kinds of papers around his desk while punching numbers into his textbook sized calculator and said this to me: "You need to get a 95% or better on the final to get a final grade of a C. That is the only way you will be able to advance. If that doesn't happen, we will see you next fall so you can repeat the Embalming 101 course." He added, with a chuckle, "Good luck with that."

I take the news and I know there is only one thing I must do. I have to get a 100% on the final. There are only three weeks left in the semester. I told some of my classmates the news. They all asked, "What are you going to do?" I told them, "I'm going to get a 100% on the final." To which they replied, "Yeah Right," "No Way," along with a lot of other confidence building comments.

Well, I got a 95% on the final, got that C as my final grade, and was able to advance and graduate on time! It was the first time in my life I really felt like I had the *will* to do something. I was surprised and shocked that I actually pulled it off. It was a life-changing experience for me. I know it doesn't sound like much, but it was a defining moment in my life. It made me feel strong and it also taught me not to get myself in that situation ever again. It taught me how to prepare for something. Being prepared is one of the most important things you can do for yourself. As it is often said, "Good Luck" is when opportunity meets preparedness.

This lesson served me well when I had to face beating something as big as cancer. You must prepare yourself, and you must educate yourself. Watch the movies, go online, join clubs, and find out how other people are beating this disease. Get yourself into a community group. Perhaps you will find folks who are much worse off than you, and they are winning the battle. I realize that a lot of people do succumb to cancer, but just as many people are beating it and going on to living happy, healthy, and long lives.

I went on to get my funeral director's license and I finally start making some pretty good money. Thank God, it was just what I needed. I'd been a "broke ass bitch" for way too long.

I had put music on the back burner for some time now. My folks were happy; all my relatives were happy and relieved. I was finally somebody. Everyone felt I was finally part of society. I was wearing a suit every day, my hair was neatly trimmed, I had my own apartment in Long Island and my car was not some old broken-down piece of shit. Everyone was happy. Except for me.

I was working my ass off. I had lost all my friends because of my work schedule. My music career was pretty much non-existent because of my work schedule. I had no girlfriend because of my work schedule. I had some money saved, but to me it seemed like my life was going nowhere. Deep down I felt like a failure. This corporate life of getting up early every day and working for a paycheck just wasn't for me. I had to develop an escape plan. Escape from the rigors of grey-suit, black-tie Corporate America and be free. It really works for some people, but it's just not my thing.

I do feel that being a funeral director is a meaningful position in life. You are there for people in their time of need. You are helping many people in the community where you live when they need you most. It was like that when I was working for a family-owned funeral home.

Back in the late 1980s and all the way through the 1990s these large corporations started buying up all the local funeral homes all over the country. It really ruined it for me. They would come down on the directors and they would want you to push sales and push families to upgrade caskets and services from time to time. I just couldn't bring myself to do it. I found it to be unethical and it really bothered me deep down. When you are a funeral director, there is a human element that goes along with the job. It seemed like that part of the job had all but disappeared. It was all about making quotas and getting bonuses.

I still keep my funeral director's license active and up to date. I have friends who own local funeral homes and I do help them out from time to time and I enjoy doing so. These days I have my own schedule and I help if I am available.

By the late 1990s I had quit my job in NY and moved to Florida. All my friends were moving down there, one by one. My parents had moved down to Florida around 1993. I had aunts and uncles and cousins and friends down in Florida. So, I moved to Florida and enrolled in college for a second time. This time it was for a degree in music.

Things were changing again. I was a lot happier and I liked it. I had gotten a steady gig in a local theater company playing bass in a show called "Always, Patsy Cline". Life was real different for me in Florida. I had some steady band gigs too. I was in school and I had my own place and it was all good.

That's when I met Karene. She was the bartender at a local club where I used to work playing in the house band. She had her daughter Mariah who was 4 years old at the time and we all got along just fine. After a few years of dating, I moved in with them. I never lived with a girlfriend before. It didn't make sense to me; it still doesn't. Why on Earth would I want to compromise my lifestyle with someone who is not my wife? But this was different. I really fell for her and the feeling was mutual. I never even dated a girl who had a child. If we were going to get serious, I figured we should all live together for a year or so, just to see if I could handle it. Everything went well. She was bartending and I was gigging, and her mom was watching Mariah at night while we were working. We both worked and we were saving money. We then decided that our 900 sq.ft., 2nd floor apartment was getting too small, so we decided to buy a house. However, there was one big problem – neither one of us could qualify for a mortgage. So, just like that, I was back to working as a funeral director. On the books, health insurance, and all that "American Dream" type of stuff. Ok, I said to myself, I will work just until we get the mortgage. Then I can go back to gigging full time. Well, that did not happen. I continued to work full time and gig part time for the better part of thirteen years. I felt now that I had a child in my life, I had to man up because it was my responsibility to raise her. I didn't take any chances while she was in school. The health insurance was in place and the money was being saved for her college. I guess it was time to finally grow up. Hell, I was forty-one years old for God's sake! I won't lie, it was a struggle in the beginning, but it was all worth it and it is all good.

After we bought the house, Karene and I figured we should get married. It just seemed like the right thing to do. I never thought of myself as a marrying kind of guy. But it did feel right, so we got married! We had an awesome wedding and all our friends and relatives and the most important people in our lives were there. It was the best day of my life! No one was going to bring me down, and no one did.

The next thing to do was to adopt Mariah. Again, it was another best day of my life. We all felt like we were a real family, especially Mariah. Finally, we all had the same last name and it felt good for all of us. This was the best move I had ever made in my life and it still is.

The relationship between the three of us remains strong and positive to this day. My having been diagnosed with cancer really had an effect on our little family. Even though I was the one with the disease, we all went through it together. If it wasn't for Karene and Mariah, I am not sure I would be here today telling you my story. I'm not sure I'd be here, period.

3

CHEMOTHERAPY & OTHER STUFF

The first question that comes to mind when you find out that you have cancer and you have to go through chemotherapy is, "Am I going to die?" Chemo is just the kind of word that, when you hear it, it makes you cringe. When I hear the word chemo now, it just brings back a lot of memories for me. Memories that I would like to forget.

Here is how this whole cancer thing started for me. The truth is, I just started feeling like something was wrong. I started belching, and every time I would eat something, I felt like I needed to burp. Then it got worse, and then it started happening randomly. My body was trying to tell me something was wrong, and I started listening to it.

It was January, the beginning of a new year. At the time I was taking medicine for acid reflux, medicine for high cholesterol and medicine for high blood pressure. I had been taking these medications every single day for over 10 years! I really didn't think much of it at the time. It seems like everybody I know is on some type of medication. It's the American way; everyone is taking this stuff and they all seem to be fine to me.

In spite of taking the acid reflux medicine, my heartburn was getting pretty bad. I started losing weight and I was feeling weak. My wife suggested I pay the doctor a visit. I went to a gastroenterologist, and he suggested I get blood work done. No problem, they take the blood and then a few days later he calls and tells me I need to come in for an ultrasound and a CT scan. The blood test results show that my white blood cell count is high. Ok, so I schedule the tests, and the following week I am getting the ultrasound. The results are that my spleen is "elevated". So now I am getting pretty concerned. I don't even know what having an elevated spleen means. I don't even know what the spleen does! Who cares about what I don't know; I do know that this doesn't sound like good news.

I am waiting for my insurance company to approve me for the CT scan. No word from them. It's been seven days since I applied for the approval and I still don't have it. This is crazy, and I am starting to feel uncomfortable about it. I realize that I have to step in and take control of this situation (if you are not on top of your own healthcare, no one is going to take care of it for you). I start making all the necessary calls. Calls to the insurance company, calls to the imaging center, calls to the doctor's office. Organizing conference calls and getting everyone on the phone at the same time so we can figure all of this out. After way too much hassle, I finally get my approval for the CT scan.

Right after I got approved, the imaging center calls me within 30 minutes and schedules me for a CT scan in two hours! I dropped whatever I was doing and went for the scan.

The truth finally did come out. My original request for the CT scan was made on a Friday afternoon. The request was sent to an approval person who did not come to work that Monday. It just got lost in a slew of other things that needed to be approved. I did get an apology from the insurance company, but the truth is, I could have died while waiting for this approval to come through.

The next morning, at 9 a.m., the phone rings. It's Dr. Towbin's office. The nice girl on the other end of the phone says that the doctor needs to see me right away, as they found something abnormal in the CT scan – but there is nothing available until 2pm! What!? She says, "Don't ask me, I'm just the receptionist. You are going to have to speak to the doctor to find out about your results."

For most of the day, Karene and I walk circles around the house, not saying a word to each other, waiting for 2 p.m. The time finally arrives. We are sitting in the doctor's office waiting for the news. Is he coming? WTF? We are waiting and waiting. Finally, in walks Dr. Towbin. He tells us that I have an intussusception. This is a condition in which part of the intestine telescopes into itself. It can be fatal if not treated, and there are fewer than 20,000 cases per year in the United States. The only fix for me is emergency surgery, as I am about 24 hours away from a total blockage. He tells Karene to take me directly to the emergency room to be admitted!

Here is where things get really peculiar. She drops me off at the emergency room, which is across town. Then, she has to drive all the way back to the other side of town to pick up the disc that my CT scan is on. Then she has to meet me back at the hospital.

They are all real great there at Bethesda Memorial Hospital in Boynton Beach, Florida. I notice that the staff and all the people are being what seems unusually nice and attentive. If you have ever gone to the emergency room, you may know what I mean when I say, "unusually nice." I wait in the emergency room for hours. Karene puts a post on Facebook, and the comments and the well-wishes start rolling in. My good friend, Jesse Finklestein, who owns Blues Radio International, hears the news and comes to visit me in the ER.

They finally find me a room. It's getting really late, so I send Karene and Jesse home. I am lying in the emergency room bed, and a couple of aides come in and start rolling me down the hallway to my room, and then back out and down another hallway, and an elevator, then another hallway. Where the hell are they taking me? Then I see the sign. Oncology. What is going on here? Do I have cancer? Is that even possible?

In walks the surgeon, Dr. Mariano Faresi. He sits at my bedside, and before he says anything, I ask him, "Do I have cancer?" "Oh no," he says, "this is the only bed available." I look to my right and I see an empty bed. "Are you sure I don't have cancer?" "No, you're going to be fine. We are going to go in and straighten out this problem you are having. Somehow you must have twisted up your colon by maybe lifting something. Or perhaps you bent yourself in the wrong way. No worries. I do this all the time and you are going to be fine. We will operate in the morning. Get some rest. Tomorrow is going to be a big day." "Okay, cool," I said. I truly believe him. I am feeling relieved; thank goodness I don't have cancer. Now, I realize that maybe not knowing at this point was for the best. I guess it was just a coincidence that I wound up in the Oncology Unit.

The next day, at 5:30 a.m., a new set of hospital aides come into the room and wheel me down to where I get prepped for the operation. In walks Dr. Faresi. Everyone is in a great mood. The operating room staff is joking and laughing, and this makes me very comfortable. The truth is I am kind of relieved that they all seem like they know what they are doing and have obviously done it before.

Since this whole thing started, they looked for a problem and they found it. They all know what it is, and they know how to fix it. Thank goodness for that. For me, the worst possible news is having the doctor say, "We are not really sure what is going on here." So,

I am feeling pretty grateful for that.

After the operation, I am in the hospital for 10 days in recovery. Every day, there are many doctors walking into my room, and they are all telling me how great I am doing. They are telling me how successful the operation was, and how I am going to be just fine in a couple of weeks. But I never see Dr. Faresi, the head surgeon. Finally, the day comes when I am to be released and go home. All I can think about is how horrible this situation was for me, and how glad I am to be going home to finish my recovery. And how glad I'll be when this whole episode of my life is behind me.

Before I can get released, the nurses tell me that the doctor is going to come in and talk to me, and he will have to sign my final release form. I'm thinking to myself, "Okay, cool. I will be out of here in no time."

It's about 7:30 a.m., and Dr. Faresi walks in and sits by my bedside. He does the normal doctor stuff. He listens to my heartbeat, reads my charts, and so on. Then he pulls up a chair next to my bed and he says, "There is something you must know. You have cancer. I'm sorry. A cancerous tumor attached itself to the outside of your colon, and that is what caused the intussusception. This is a metastatic type of cancer and it spreads throughout the body." Then he gets up and says, "You are free to go home now, or you can wait for the oncologist. He should be here in a couple of hours." I'm stunned, I'm speechless, and I'm devastated. Dr. Faresi then hands me a folder with my results that I am to give to the Oncologist. It's full of medical jargon that I don't understand. Yet I see words like aggressive and advanced. This obviously make me very nervous.

I somehow find the strength to call Karene and tell her the news. She is at the hospital within minutes. We wait for further instruction from the medical staff. In walks a small, unassuming man in a white coat. He is obviously another doctor. He looks at his paperwork and checks the room number on the door. He looks at me and says, "Are you Mark?" "Yes," I say. With that, he gets down on one knee, takes my hand, and says, "Don't worry too much about it. You're going to be fine." He is smiling and radiant. He is confident, and for some reason I know he is telling the truth.

I don't know how or why I know this; I just know it. He gently puts my wife and me at ease. I instantly know that this doctor, who is barely five feet tall, is going to be a giant in my life.

He then tells me I need to go for testing. Karene and I are trying to be upbeat and positive about the whole situation after we get home from the hospital. It takes all week to schedule all the tests. There are all kinds of scans, bone marrow tests, blood tests, urine tests. There are tests for everything.

All appointments are finally scheduled, and all my tests are completed. The worst one was the bone marrow test. They actually go into your hip, and they take marrow out of your bone. And then they take a little bone spur out of your hip. You have to be awake; you can't be under anesthesia for that type of thing. It's pretty intense. It's not fun. Kind of like chemo, and it hurts like a bitch.

There's not much fun stuff in this chapter, that's for sure.

After I do all my testing, it's time to wait for the results. From the day I find out I have cancer to the day I actually get all my test results back is a 21-day waiting period. So, get this: you have this huge operation, you go home with the news that you have cancer, and you spend a week doing invasive testing. And then you wait. You wait... and you wait some more. At least it seems like that. I know, 21 days is not the end of the world. But when you're waiting for that kind of news, it just seems to take a longer time than it should.

So, we became friendly with a nurse over at the nearby Lantana Oncology and Hematology Center. Her name is Sandy. She calls me one day and says, "I'm your nurse navigator. Let me know if there's anything that you need." I was stunned. I guess when you get cancer, you find there's a different level of health care. There's a difference because, I think, they're dealing with life and death on a daily basis. Everyone, I mean *everyone*, that I came into contact with in the industry was just awesome. All the nurses, all the doctors, the staff, everybody. So, Sandy would call me and give me little glimpses of hope. "It looks good," she'd say about my test results. "I think it's going to be okay." You know, really helping me out psychologically with that kind of stuff. She was one of the nicest people I have ever met. Sandy is a 25-year breast cancer survivor.

The day comes when I have to find out where things stand. I'm in the waiting room holding Karene's hand, and then we walk in. You don't know if this is going to be Stage I, II, III, or IV, or if the cancer has spread here or spread there. Am I going to have to start making funeral plans for myself? It's crazy. It's like a million thoughts are running through your mind at the same time. If the news is bad, how am I going to handle it?

Dr. Eduardo Garcia walks in the room and says, "So, the news is that it's Stage II and the cancer did not spread, and it all stayed below the diaphragm." You see, Non-Hodgkin's Lymphoma is the kind of cancer that gives you those big lumps. You know, under your arms, in your groin, and in your neck. And once you start noticing lumps, it's usually bad and probably stage IV. It is a stroke of luck that it was found in its early stages. Dr. Garcia said that there was only one tumor, and that is what caused my colon to collapse. So, I got lucky in that way.

The doctor said, "The plan now is you must do six rounds of chemotherapy. We need to make sure we got it all. If you don't do the chemotherapy, we're looking at a 50/50 chance that this is going to come back; this is going to get you. It could be three years; it could be five years. It's on a cellular level, you see?" They had to kill the white cells, because it's a white blood cell disease. They kill as many as they possibly can – without killing the patient. And then the body will rejuvenate new, healthy white blood cells.

That's the idea behind it. So, as your white blood

cells are being killed off, you're starting to feel worse and worse. Because you're dying a little bit. If the cells are dying, the body is dying. All you really are is your cells, you know?

Chemotherapy? Should I do it? It is all up to me. My doctor suggests it, my family suggests it, and you know, I also think it's a good idea. In reality, I really did. We had a good friend of ours deal with his cancer the holistic way, a musician and a great guy, and it didn't work. The holistic way just didn't work for him. We had conversations and talked about it and I knew that it was my turn now. What call was I going to make? For me, doing the modern medicine route made more sense.

Still, not doing chemotherapy is just as courageous as actually doing chemotherapy. It's a personal choice. I don't question anybody in this position who declines it. You have to do what's right for you. You have to do what works in your life, and for your life. It just happened to be my own personal decision to go forward with it.

The big day is April 19th. That is the day of my first chemotherapy treatment. I can't really remember what I did the night before, but I know I didn't get much sleep. Karene and I had to pack snacks and water. We packed up extra blankets and pillows. We were trying to mentally prepare ourselves for this. I was scheduled to receive chemotherapy treatments every 21 days. Every 21st day, I got stuck with needles, and injected with 10 bags of chemotherapy drugs. Five are different chemo drugs, and five are to reduce the side effects.

There was a time I could have told you what the names of the drugs were, but I have since blocked them out of my memory. I remember we arrived there around 10 a.m. and left around 4:30 p.m. Karene was with me every step of the way. It's a slow drip, slow drip, slow drip. It's crazy. I can't believe I'm in this position.

I sit in the chair just hoping to fall asleep. No chance, my mind is racing like mad. Crazy thoughts are running through my head. Reality is setting in; I can't believe I am in this position. I start wondering, pondering all different kinds of questions. Is this something that I brought on myself? Is this something that happened to me from bad eating habits? Have I been drinking too much? Do I have too much stress in my life? I also start thinking about conspiracy theories. Is the food we are eating being tainted by big corporations? Is the American government slowly poisoning its citizens? All kinds of thoughts were running through my head. What if they are true?

I found that if I didn't take control of the thoughts inside my head, those thoughts would soon take control of me! They could possibly create a false sense of paranoia. That is a very real side effect of having a cancer diagnosis. Having cancer is not only physically tough, it is also psychologically very tough. So, in a lot of ways, this is really where my psychological fight began. I felt as if I had no choice. I had to become mentally stronger. So, I did, and this seems to serve me well in my post cancer life.

4

THE BLUES

Let's talk a little bit about the blues. How the blues can affect one's life. How the blues affects my life.

Right now, I'm sitting in a parking lot, talking into my iPhone. I'm about to go into Leftovers Café, this little restaurant in Jupiter, Florida. I play guitar here a couple times a month, singing and strumming the blues on my acoustic guitar. They have great food, and the staff is real nice. They want me to play through the house PA system. I prefer my own, but I go through theirs so they can pump the music outside as well. It's a nice easy gig. They like me, I like them, all is good.

I was working at Leftover's before I got sick. I had a bunch of dates on the books but had to call them up and tell them I was sick and wouldn't be back for a while. And they were totally cool, saying, "All right, just let us know when you're ready to come back." I called them afterward and got a whole new string of dates. Everything I wanted and then some. They even hired my full band for some nights.

So, I show up here and play my acoustic blues. Families walk by, and I don't really know what they think of it. You know, back in the 1960s and the 1970s and even the 1980s, if I was able to play the acoustic guitar the way I'm playing it these days, I think I would've amassed a pretty nice audience of people to come and see me play. Like I said before, sometimes I feel like I am more a novelty rather than a professional musician. You know, I'm the guy who's fingerpicking on the little guitar with a tweed amplifier. Shit, I must be a blues man. It's as if I'm doing an act, or something like that. Let me tell you something, this is no act, this is what I love to do, this is my life's work, this is who I am, and this is who I have always been.

This is who I have always been? A thought just occurs to me. *Is* this who I have always been? Well, as I think about it a little, the true answer is, Yeah, I think so? No… wait… I'm *sure* this is who I have always been. It certainly isn't how I have always lived, but it *is* who I have always been.

I did a lot of soul searching while I was getting my chemotherapy treatments. I would think about the past a lot. I would think about my deceased father and mother. I often wonder how devastating the news of me being stricken with cancer would have been for them.

My mother died of esophageal cancer one year before I was diagnosed. My father has been gone 10 years at this point.

I thought a lot about life in general. I thought about how much I have to live for. I would think about how much I love my wife, how much I love my daughter, my sister, my niece and my nephew. I just knew I had to beat it.

I had so many folks watching this all go down on Facebook. I started posting this whole thing from the very minute it began. Even before I was diagnosed with Non-Hodgkin's Lymphoma, it seemed like the whole blues community was watching this on Facebook. I had thousands of people watching me and there was no way I was going to let them down. I didn't even realize that I was that popular, apparently due, in part, to all of the connections I have made being the host of the Monday Night Jam at The Funky Biscuit in Boca Raton, Florida and, of course, social media. I'll get more into that in the next chapter. From those two things alone, it's fair to say I have an actual fan base, or as I prefer to think of it, friends.

Which brings me back to the blues and the blues community. The Blues Foundation is an organization that commits itself to keeping the blues alive and maintaining the true tradition of this American art form from its beginnings up until present day. There are many facets to this community and one of them is the HART FUND. The Hart Fund is run by Dr. Janice

Johnson who is an extraordinary woman who donates her time and commits herself to helping others. I want you all to know that this organization helped me out with my medical bills. Not only can cancer kill you, it sure can take a nice chunk out of your wallet! I just want to thank the Hart Fund for helping me out, and for helping out thousands of people who are in need. It never would've happened if it weren't for the blues.

That's what things are like in my world. It's very strange and very sad, how much less important music seems to have become over the years. Back in the late 1960s all the way through the 1980s, music seemed to bond a whole generation of people together. It's just not like that anymore.

I recently bought a car from a very mature 22-year-old young man working in the dealership. He asked me what I did for a living. I said I was a musician, and I play the blues. He replied: "The blues? What is that?" I nearly fell on the floor. It made me sad.

When I grew up, rock music was the center of our lives and I got most of my blues from guys like Eric Clapton, Jimmy Page and John Mayall. You defined yourself by your record collection, or the concerts you went to, the clothes you would wear, and your hair (it's always been about the hair for some reason)!

I remember the very first record I ever got. It was "Déjà vu" by Crosby, Stills, Nash & Young. It was one of my favorite records. It still is. Far from the blues, but I love the vocal harmonies. Graham Nash and Neil Young could sing so high, it was just phenomenal. I really liked it because you were really hearing the voices of the singers and the instruments of the musicians.

In a lot of popular music today, we hear more of the work of the producers and engineers more than the singers and musicians. Digital programs and studios make everything so perfect today. With vocal harmonizers and drum machines, everything is quantized. Nowadays, folks are making records in their bedrooms that sound perfect.

For me, it's those little imperfections that made some of those old records so great. I think that is one of the reasons I am attracted to blues music. Not only the old stuff, but the modern stuff too.

Growing up in New York, it really wasn't a mecca for the blues. It was all about Southern rock for a time, and then it was all about classic rock. Or was it the other way around? Classic rock was Led Zeppelin, Bad Company, The Who, the Rolling Stones, the Eagles. That was all on the radio; good stuff. Not much blues, though.

I didn't really get exposed to the blues until I started going out to this club in Long Island. There was a band that played there, Little Buster & the Soul Brothers. It was the only band in town that had black people in it. It seemed like every other band that was playing the clubs in Long Island were just some neighborhood kids from the suburbs with a guitar and a cool haircut. But, Buster, he was a bluesman; he could sing the shit out of a soul tune like it was nobody's business. He was blind as a bat, but man, he could play that guitar and sing those blues and Motown songs. The bass player was badass; the horn players were unbelievable. And they did a mixture of soul music, Motown music, and blues. At that time, I didn't even know there was a difference between blues music, soul music, and Motown – but it was all great stuff.

They were playing music by the Temptations, Sam & Dave, and Otis Redding. They were doing some really great stuff. One night, they invited me up to sing, and I sang "Steamroller Blues" by James Taylor. That was the only blues song I knew! And it was because, well, James Taylor did it. You know, if you were an acoustic-strumming guy, you had to know some JT songs. So, I did it, and they looked at me and said, "Oh man, you can do this. You have that voice, that feel." And I was thinking, "Thanks for the compliment, but there is no way I can do this." I didn't have very much self-confidence back then. I was probably in my mid-20s. I was into this classic rock thing, and was doing glam band music, covers of Poison, Bon Jovi, all that stuff. I guess I was just another kid from the neighborhood with a guitar and a cool haircut.

It wasn't until I was in my late 30s that I started really getting into the blues. I had moved to South Florida and there was this club that opened up in a little town named Lake Worth, The Bamboo Room, a blues club. I knew the manager, and at the time, they had hired a guy named Keith Brown to be the resident blues man. He was an acoustic guitar player. They said he was the son of a sharecropper from Mississippi. He was the real deal, and they were going to put an acoustic band together.

They had this upright bassist from a neighboring town who wasn't working out, so I got the call and joined the band. It was Keith on vocals and guitar, me on upright bass, and a young kid named Jason Ricci playing harmonica. Jason went on to become a world-class harmonica player, a Blues Music Awards winner, a Grammy winner. What a guy. It's a pleasure to know him and call him a friend. We still play together occasionally, 20 years later. He's a little crazy, and an amazing musician. He goes real deep and takes the instrument where no one else has ever taken it. In my opinion, Jason is one of the best in the world, if not the best.

I was getting older. The difference between being a younger guy and an older guy is that when greatness walks into your life and you're older, you know it. When you're young and greatness walks into your life, you might not recognize it as greatness. You might recognize it as just another guy or something. But Jason was great. He's always the star of the show, even to this day, no matter who he gets on stage with. And the cool thing about him is that he doesn't try to be the star of the show. He just is.

So, there I was, playing my upright, which I normally don't do a lot of these days. I'm being introduced to music by Furry Lewis, Slim Harpo, Skip James, Son House, Robert Johnson, Blind Willie McTell, Tommy Johnson, Leroy Carr, Keb' Mo'. He's one of my favorites who I've actually met up with a few times. Taj Mahal, another great. All the great acoustic guitar blues guys. Mississippi Fred McDowell,

Mississippi John Hurt, Blind Boy Fuller, Blind Blake, Blind Wille Johnson (makes me wonder sometimes if being blind doesn't open your eyes to something deeper that the rest of us are missing), Lightnin' Hopkins, and the list goes on and on. We did all this great acoustic blues music, and I was playing bass, and it was a phenomenal experience. It was just such a great gig. So well-done. The sound of the bass was great, and Jason didn't play through an amp. He just played clean through a vocal mic into the PA system. It was the most organic gig I think I've ever had. All acoustic, and it was just to die for.

That's how I got into the blues. I am still into it and it feels like home. However, these days I'm letting the music dictate what my next step is going to be. Hopefully I'll find an audience somehow, some way. I think the day of the rock star is dead anyway. If I spend the rest of my life playing in cafés, restaurants, local bars, and the occasional blues festival, so be it. I'm still going to be fulfilled, because my life is about art. My life is about the blues, and the blues is my art.

5

BOHEMIAN RHAPSODY

"Bohemian Rhapsody." Wow, what a song. Everybody knows it, everybody I know grew up listening to it, a lot of young people know it. Everybody sings along with it; everybody knows the words. It's a song that really connects with people for some reason. Maybe it's because there is something for everyone in that song. There's the singer/songwriter type of intro. There is an instrumental section, there is a hard rock section, and there is even an opera section. It's recorded extremely well, and everybody I know loves it.

I can remember when the song first came out. I was a kid, and I'd never heard anything like it before. My mom used to listen to the radio a lot in those days. The radio was a fixture in the little ranch-style house where my family lived in Massapequa Park, Long Island, New York. It was a little house right in the heart of suburbia where the radio took up permanent residence on the kitchen counter, and it was always on.

The kitchen was the center of our home. All of life's major decisions went down in the kitchen. Particularly on the kitchen table. All the bills got paid on the kitchen table. All the mail was opened on the kitchen table. Every report card was opened up and read at the kitchen table. I got an allowance of two dollars a week, which was given to me at the kitchen table. Every punishment I ever got was delivered to me sitting across from my father at the kitchen table. Every decision that ever had to be made, no matter how big or how small, happened on or around that kitchen table. No one I knew had an office, or even a desk. It was the kitchen table. Every new thing, every gadget acquired, was opened up at the kitchen table.

I remember we once got a calculator when they first came out. It was made by Texas Instruments. You had to plug it in. It was a big, big deal. It was opened up at the kitchen table. We got an electric typewriter made by IBM. We had one of the real old ones before that; it came with the black metal case. An electric typewriter was like the future, man! It was unpackaged on the kitchen table. The truth is, even with all the good things that happened around the kitchen table, I hated sitting around that fucking table. I got emotionally beat up by my dad daily sitting at that table, and it went on for years and years.

The radio was how we got the most current news: the weather, school closings, and music. That was the music of our lives. Casey Kasem's Top 40, and man, my mom sure did love Casey Kasem. She loved the Top 40.

I clearly remember when "Bohemian Rhapsody" was playing on the radio, and they were playing the heck out of it. My mom would start singing along. "Mama Mia, Mama Mia...." Oh, that was funny. My mom used to love to sing. She'd sing everything. She sang until the day she died.

There wasn't any blues, or jazz, or anything like that on AM radio. AM radio stations were mostly talk radio. There were a few stations that would play the popular music of the day. The AM radio stations did not play any Muddy Waters, or Howlin' Wolf, or B.B. King, or Hendrix, or Led Zeppelin, or Bad Company. That is what the FM radio stations were for. They would play rock music. Which is known today as classic rock, but back then it was just rock. Anything hangs around long enough and it's a classic. Every once in a while, an FM station would have a blues hour at two o'clock in the morning or something like that.

We never listened to rock music in my house or in the car until I was about 16 years old. As a kid we had one family car. My dad drove all the time. We all listened to whatever my dad wanted to listen to. It was the same with the TV. We all watched whatever my dad wanted to watch on TV. It wasn't just our household; all the families on our block, and in the rest of the neighborhood, were in the same situation. Whatever dad wanted to watch, that is what the family watched. It was just normal life back then. Nobody I knew had a TV or a phone in their bedroom. The house had one phone, and everybody shared it, and if you were lucky you had an extension.

I really believe that listening to that old radio in the kitchen would bring my mom back to a time when she was younger, before TV, when things were real simple. It's hard to imagine a world without television. Nowadays, I walk into a bar to do a gig, and there are way too many TVs blasting sports, and each one is on a different channel. That's how it is today, but back when my mom was a kid, nobody had a television, especially in the kitchen! The radio was king, and it was the centerpiece of the family room. My mom used to tell me stories of how the family would sit around the living room and listen to radio shows like "The Shadow". She said it was better than television because it forced you to use your imagination. I believe she may have been right.

I remember one year my dad did manage to scrape up a few bucks for a television and stereo combo. This baby was a serious piece of furniture. It had an enormous 19in. screen and it was a color TV! It was proudly placed in the main living room and when it was new, I was not allowed to touch it. Forget about portability, it was big, and it was heavy. The cabinet was made of real oak wood. It was also full of records. You could stack up to 10 records on it and it would only play one side, and then another record would drop and so on. This was high tech stuff for the time. All the records we had were of all the old crooners like Dean

Martin, Frank Sinatra, Bing Crosby and so on. The only rock records we had were "Meet the Beatles" and one Motown record by the Supremes. I remember when the TV broke. There was this guy who lived around the corner and he was the TV repair man. He would make house calls to your sick TV. Wow, things sure have changed.

Well, eventually a small 13in. black-and-white TV with seven channels replaced the radio on the kitchen counter. I don't think we ever bought another radio after that.

During my illness, I'm home alone almost every day while my wife goes to work. I am in the middle of chemotherapy treatments, and the treatments are getting tougher and tougher to handle. I start thinking about the past a whole lot during this time. I am getting so sick from the treatments and I am really questioning if I am going to live or die. At this point, I start smoking some marijuana. I used to smoke pot in high school, but then I just stopped one day. No particular reason, I'd just had enough of it. All my friends, and the nursing staff, were telling me I should try smoking some pot. It would make me feel better and take away a lot of the anxiety that is often associated with chemo treatments. So, I talk to my doctors about it. I would talk to my doctors about everything that I was eating and drinking. I really wanted to feel better, so I asked each one of them what they thought about it. They all agreed, saying, "It can't hurt you." So, I decide I am going try it.

I had not smoked pot for over 37 years, but all I had

to do was make one phone call and it was delivered to my house within the hour. I didn't even have to pay for it! It certainly was pretty easy for me to get. Especially for something that is still considered to be an illegal substance in most states. Guess being a musician still has its perks!

It was working and I was starting to feel better. I had a bit more energy and it enabled me to focus on things a bit more. I finally felt like I was getting ready to accomplish something. I had a true desire to get my mind off the horrible situation I was in and do something worthwhile, but what was I going to do? I did have a little more energy, but I still couldn't go out in public or anything like that due to the risk of infection.

One thing for sure is that I'm not going to sit around all day watching movies. I'm just not that guy. I'm a doer, I'm always doing something. So, I made a decision that every day, I would get up and accomplish something, even if it was a small task. I felt it would move me forward in life.

You see, the truth is, I just made a decision. It's as simple as that. In my mind I made a decision to beat cancer. I got myself focused on all the things I was doing. I was not going to waste this time. In my mind, I turned the whole situation around. Instead of wondering what was going to happen to me, I would visualize myself being healthy and getting back to work. Once I made that decision, everything started to change. If you change the way you look at things, the things you look at start to change. I started to become a more positive person. I started to become a more motivated person. I looked at my cancer like it was an opportunity. I know it sounds crazy, but I realized for the first time in my life that I wasn't having to run anywhere. The opportunity I had was time. Since I was a child, I had not had time off like this. I knew that for the better part of a year I had no responsibilities. I had no deadlines to meet, I had no meetings to prepare for, no meetings to attend. No gigs, no rehearsals, I did not have to clean the house, I did not have to walk the dogs, I did not have to prepare for visitors, or anything. My sole purpose in life for right now was to focus on getting healthy and putting this behind me.

I was now in my mid-50s, and I wanted to come out of this on the other side. I felt like I had a good chunk of living left to do. So, I now have to pinpoint and focus on something. What am I going to do with all this time? What am I going to accomplish? Am I actually able to come out of these treatments as a changed person? So, I think to myself, besides coming out of this with good health, which is the obvious goal, what makes sense to me? The answer: music. In some way, shape, or form, the power of music has saved my life more than once. So here we go again.

Become a better musician? That's all I could really do. I started leaving my beloved Martin 000-28 acoustic guitar out on the guitar stand that sits in my living room. It was the perfect thing for me to focus on. I also love to play the bass, but playing the upright bass is way too physical for me to do at this point. Playing the electric bass means I would have to sit in a particular place in my house and plug it into an amplifier. It would have been too much preparation for me to even get started. Given my weakened condition, the acoustic guitar made a lot more sense. You can take an acoustic guitar and sit in bed with it, sit on the couch, bring it upstairs, take it outside. And that's exactly what I did. It became my 24/7 companion. I just started going to YouTube videos and checking out some amazing guitar players.

That's when I decided to start taking guitar lessons online. I figured I would learn to play "Bohemian Rhapsody." No singing involved, just all guitar.

The decision was made! This is what I was going to do. This was going to keep me focused, and I was determined to do it, beginning to end. Sometimes I start projects and then, you know, they're left undone for some reason. But this was something that couldn't be left undone. I got into it and learned the first section of it. That took me weeks. Just to learn maybe the first 40 seconds of the song! But I figured, what else have I got to do? After I learned the first section, I learned the second, then the third. And there are eight or nine sections to this song.

I started learning the opera part. Hours and hours of practice. It's all muscle memory. But I learned how to play it, along with learning to play some other things as well. Because just learning that one song was kind of driving me crazy. But I was able to really delve into my acoustic guitar playing, and it just really helped me stay focused on something other than my illness the whole time I was sick.

I put about a year into learning this song. These days, I'm playing "Bohemian Rhapsody" at almost every gig I do with my acoustic guitar. And I've still yet to play it correctly from beginning to end!

But whenever I play it, or hear that song on the radio, it brings me right back to that old kitchen table and listening to my mom sing.

6

THE FUNKY BISCUIT

I'm sitting here on my couch, petting Lola, one of my chihuahuas. I have two little chihuahuas, Bailee and Lola, and they're both very loving. Lola is a rescue dog, and she loves her daddy and her mommy. Like all of us, she has a past. I'm not sure where she actually came from, or what she went through before we got her, but just like many people I know, she obviously has some issues. I think she's working through them slowly, and she is not as freaked out as she was when we first got her. But this chapter is not about my chihuahuas (although maybe it *should* be), it's about a nightclub named the Funky Biscuit.

The Funky Biscuit is located in Boca Raton, Florida, or shall I say, "The Biscuit," as it is affectionately known by many. It's become a big part of my life in recent years. It's a blues club that also lends itself to jam bands, tribute bands, some classic rock bands, funk bands, and the occasional jazz musician. The great thing about this club is that no matter what night of the week you go there, you will find top-notch bands and musicians regardless of the genre. Bands and musicians from all over the country are trying to get a gig at the Funky Biscuit. If you are lucky enough to land a gig there, it's a prestigious thing, especially if you are from California or Memphis or Oregon. The blues world watches what goes on in that club. It gives you some bragging rights, especially if you are from out of town.

My involvement in the Funky Biscuit went down like this. It's 2011 and a new club opens up in town, and everybody is telling me I have to go and check it out, so I go over and take a look. There's a wonderful Hammond B-3 organ on stage, a very nice drum set on a drum riser, and it is properly mic'd. There is a selection of vintage Fender guitar amplifiers and an Ampeg SVT bass rig. It is staffed with some very capable sound men. The PA system is to die for compared to any other club within hundreds of miles. If you're a local musician or just someone who loves live music, to have a club of this caliber open up in your town is a real score. And I just happen to know the sound man. He tells me to drop off a promo package and he will do his best to help me get a gig there. So, I drop off a package. I don't get the gig at first, but eventually I did get to do a few shows there. It's a beautiful room, so a lot of local bands are playing there from Monday through Thursday. And it seems like every weekend, the club is bringing in bands from out of town. So, you know, there are just very few slots available. It's all the rage. Everyone in town is talking about the Funky Biscuit.

A couple years pass by, and I am doing my local gigs on the weekends and working as a funeral director in a local funeral home during the week. I'm not really paying much attention to what was happening at The Biscuit. I am paying the mortgage on a house and raising our daughter, Mariah. She was 7 years old when Karene and I married in 2002 and one of the cutest kids you had ever seen. So, with all the responsibilities going on in my life, unfortunately there wasn't much time to really dig into the music scene.

Then I hear through the grapevine that they have this jam going on at the Biscuit on Monday nights. So, I show up one Monday night with my bass, hoping to get a chance to jam. I walk in and there's a band playing. Okay, this is cool. Then the band takes a break, and that's cool too. I'm standing there with my bass guitar, along with other musicians waiting to have an opportunity to get on stage. There were maybe 10-15 people waiting to jam on that particular night. The band goes back up, same guys, and none of us get to play. I'm thinking to myself that this is not much of a jam at all.

I don't give it much thought, and I go back to my working day job and playing in a local cover band on the weekends. Another year goes by, and then I get a phone call from the club owner, a guy named Al. Nice guy. People in the community respect him. And he says to me that David Shelley, the current host of the Monday night jam, (who was not hosting on the night I attended) has been having some health issues and he has to take some time off. Al tells me that they have been going through substitutes for David, and he wants to know if I want to host the jam for an evening.

My initial thought was that nobody ever asks a bass player to host a jam. At least not that I know of. I wonder what's up with all the guitar players? I agree to do it. I ask him if I can use my own band. He agrees, with the condition that I use his Hammond B3 player and the guitarist from the original Monday night band. It's the day after Father's Day in 2014. There is a small crowd. People who want to play, and a few folks who came down to listen to the music.

To be honest, this came at a perfect time for me. I had made the decision one week prior that I was going to leave my day job. At this point in my life, our daughter, Mariah, had graduated from high school and was off on her own. I was getting all kinds of offers to go on small tours with national and international recording artists. I was turning them all down because I was locked into this day job. I felt I could get depressed if I didn't make a change. I then get a call from Diunna Greenleaf from Houston, Texas. She needs a bass player for Europe. With encouragement from Karene, I decide to take the gig. So, I give my notice at my day job. We decide that after I get home from Europe, I can figure out how I am going to make a living. I did a couple of tours with Diunna, and it was a wonderful experience for me. I will always be grateful for that. That is how I got back into being a full-time musician again after many years, and that is when I got serious about playing the acoustic guitar.

So, after returning to Florida, I fall right back into the Funky Biscuit gig. I merge my trio with Al's guitarist and Hammond player, which I eventually inherit. It is now time to start the evening. We play a couple of blues tunes, and then I start to get people up on stage. A bass player comes up for a couple songs, and I get to walk off stage to check out which musicians are in the house. A guitarist wants to come up, so he plays a couple songs. Then there were drummers who wanted to get on stage. At all times, I'm mixing and matching players, and three-and-a-half hours go by pretty quickly.

It was fun for me. I liked it, and I guess word spread, since I got to continue hosting the jam. More people started showing up. There were a lot of players and listeners. All of a sudden, we became a real community. A packed house at the Funky Biscuit every Monday night. After three months, it felt like a Saturday night, and I ended up with the full-time gig as the Monday night host. At this point, we decided to do something different. I began to book a "Featured Artist" each week. The jam was going good, going strong. Real strong, for about three years.

Then I got sick. When that happened, everything changed, as it does for everyone who winds up with cancer. I had to take about five weeks off for my operation. My good friend Richie took my place as the host, and my good friend Chuck came in to take my place on bass. Before I started the chemo, I asked my doctor if I could work. "Yeah, sure," he said, "you can work while you are in treatment. Just take it easy." I thought to myself, "Wow, that is awesome."

As I've said earlier, I started the chemotherapy treatments on April 19th. For the first six days after my first treatment, I actually felt pretty good. I had a headache the night after treatment and that was it. I went to bed, and then I woke up the next day feeling pretty good. I was feeling better and getting stronger every day. I'm thinking to myself, "I can do this." Doctor Garcia told me that I would feel okay for about five days and then it would hit me. I would start to feel run down and lethargic. It's now day six after my treatment and I am actually feeling very good. I figure that next week I can go back to hosting the Monday night jam! It is now 10 days after my treatment. I still don't feel run down or lethargic like the doctor said, so I give the club a call and tell them I am fine, I am ready to get back to work. It is now 12 days after my treatment, and I show up at the Biscuit. I'm getting tons of hugs and kisses from everyone there. There are more than 200 people in attendance. The house band has now been named "The Funky Biscuit Allstars," and we kick off the evening with some great blues. There was some real excitement in the air, especially for me. I'm finally back, I'm feeling strong, and I am ready to do this. I have this chemotherapy thing under control, and I am going to beat cancer!

The next morning, I wake up and I'm not feeling so great. The flu is going around, and I am just hoping that I didn't catch anything. I am aware that my immune system is probably compromised, and I was careful to disinfect all the microphones the night before. As the day went on, I started feeling worse and worse. I was convinced that I had gotten the flu. That evening, when Karene came home, she suggested that we go to the emergency room just to be on the safe side. I agreed, and off we went, back to the hospital. They took us in, and I gave them my story. I told them that I already know the flu is going around and that is probably what I have. And I know this because I googled it. Ha! The nurse looked at me and laughed, and said, "Dr. Google sends a lot of people to emergency." The nice nurse then says, "How about we start by taking some blood and we will let you know, if you have the flu, sir." I said okay and then I shut up!

Here is how all this went down. Thirteen days after my first round of chemotherapy, I wound up in the hospital. My WBC (white blood cell count) went down to 800. A normal WBC is somewhere between 5,000 and 10,000. With only an 800 WBC, I was in serious danger. We are all made up of cells. Your hair, skin, eyes, everything is made of cells. If a person's cells are dying, then the person is dying as a result. Needless to say, I felt like I was dying.

I was admitted back into the hospital that evening and remained there for the next five days in quarantine. I was being injected with liquid antibiotics. IV bags loaded with chemicals were just being pumped into my body. I had a real bad infection. This was pretty tough emotionally for me. The seriousness of having cancer is not something you should fool around with. It actually is a matter of life and death. As I lay there, feeling lonesome in the hospital, I could not help but think I needed to make some serious decisions about my life. My first decision was, "I cannot afford to take any more chances with my health."

So, I left the Biscuit gig. I left all my gigs. I cancelled more than 140 of them.

My good friend Richie took over as jam host in my absence. He is a great guitar player, singer, and a great guy. Everybody loves Richie, as do I.

Al, the owner of the Biscuit, says Richie will be taking my place as the jam host only until I come back. I thought to myself, "That is very nice, but weird to get back a gig after seven months." I figured I was not even going to give it a second thought at this time. I would deal with it when the time comes. I followed what was happening on Monday nights at the Biscuit on Facebook. A lot of people would take live Facebook videos of the bands that were playing, and there were tons of comments. I continued to book the Monday night jam's "Featured Artist" from my bedroom. I really needed to do something of value while I was home for such an extended period of time. It really helped me feel connected to what was happening in the outside world – as I lay on my bed without a speck of hair on my body!

The club had asked me if I was going to set up a GoFundMe page to help with my living and medical expenses. I told them I didn't want to do that. You see, I'm not that guy. I never want something for nothing, and I get real embarrassed if I have to ask anybody for anything. I'm afraid they might look at me as some kind of loser or something. I've always worked pretty hard to get through some stuff. I just don't want to be viewed that way. I figured Karene and I would just bite the bullet financially, and if we had to take on some debt, we would. With any luck, we would eventually end up working our way out of debt. We would just do what we had to do. We'd done it before, so we could do it again. It sucks, but it can be done.

So, I tell Karene that I wasn't crazy about the idea. She said I was crazy. She said that there are people out there who want to help. There are also many folks who have the means to help. "Maybe the Funky Biscuit should put up the GoFundMe page," she said. "It would be a big help." We never spoke about it again.

After a few weeks had gone by, I hadn't even given it a second thought. Then one Sunday morning, we were sitting up in bed, having coffee and petting the dogs. Karene opened the computer and there it was! The Funky Biscuit had started a GoFundMe page! I felt kind of funny about the whole thing. I guess you could say I had mixed feelings. Truthfully, I was happy that it was there, but I was kind of embarrassed by it at first. But there was also a sense of relief. You know, as a musician, if you don't work, you don't get paid. After the first day that the GoFundMe page was live, I could I see that this music community really started to step up. They really began to support me.

It was one of the most humbling experiences of my life. There were hundreds of donations. The Biscuit raised $18,000 on that page alone. I mean, to me that's a lot of money for folks to give you just because you are sick. It's really amazing, and that's just one of the reasons I love being part of the blues world. The folks who are in it are some of the nicest people I have ever met in my life. You know, with house bills coming up, and car payments, insurance, medical bills, everything coming in, that kind of money was a big deal, and it really helped.

I'm pretty lucky because I get a lot of publicity by hosting this Monday night jam. The Biscuit is constantly promoting on Facebook, Instagram, Twitter, etc. They also have an enormous mailing list. The social media guys there are just awesome. They consistently use great graphics and they are constantly putting out posters for bands or events that they are hosting. It seems like someone is on social media 24 hours a day, seven days a week. They do it all, and thanks to them, many people in the blues world at least knew my name. Not everyone, but I am sure it was a big help, and I owe it all to the Funky Biscuit. They're the ones who gave me the push.

It was Monday, September 25th. That was the first date that I was well enough to come back to work. So, I booked myself as the "Featured Artist" for that night.

The place was packed. I walked into the club and immediately received a standing ovation. That made me feel really good, and I just knew it was going to be a good night. I could just feel it in the air. It seemed like everyone I ever knew was there. It was a very surreal moment for me. All my friends were there. There was just an endless flow of people walking through the door. Some folks were carrying guitars, some were carrying other instruments. Some other folks were just coming in to socialize and dig some good music. They were coming in groups. I really couldn't have asked for more. I still can't wrap my head around the large number of folks who were interested in my well-being.

After I said hello to what seemed like over a couple hundred people, I walked on the stage to set up my bass. Everything was exactly the way I left it. I walked up to the bass rig and plugged in my instrument. I plucked a few notes, and easily found myself a decent sound, and it felt like I never left. I was right back in the swing of things, and it felt good.

I was informed that Richie was going to be a permanent member of the Monday Night Funky Biscuit Allstars! That was exactly what I was hoping for. Now Richie and I get to jam together every Monday night. I couldn't be happier about that decision.

Before the band is about to walk on stage, Al says he wants to talk to me in the office. I walk in and I get the welcome back hug and handshake. Boy, that felt good. Then he gives me a large manila envelope and tells me to open it. I slowly undo the little wire like tab, and I look inside. I can't believe what I see. My mouth is open, and my jaw hits the floor. The envelope is full of cash! Hundred-dollar bills, fifty-dollar bills and twenty-dollar bills. I say, "What is this?" His answer was, "This is for you. I decided to pay you for every night that you missed." That kind of generosity and love can bring you to tears, my friend.

I guess when you get cancer or any life-threatening disease, it can, and it really does bring out the best in others. Especially for those that are close to you. If those around you see you are keeping a positive attitude, if they see you being optimistic in the face of such adversity, they start to recognize the blessings that they have in their own lives.

So, thank you, Al, and everyone else who reached out to help me. I will never forget your generosity and your friendship!

7

CANCER CAN ROCK

I want to tell you about a guy I know. His name is Jay Rubin. I know Jay from the Funky Biscuit. He is a big-time music fan and he goes out almost every night to see all his favorite bands, mostly blues bands. He goes to a ton of blues festivals, blues cruises, and blues clubs. You can find him in Memphis for the Blues Music Awards and the International Blues Challenge. He is a great supporter of the blues community, he is a great guy, and he is "in the know."

I woke up one Sunday morning, a few months into my treatments, and I saw that Jay sent me a video of a woman named Cathy Ponton King. She was singing a fantastic song. There was a video interview with her as well. Everything was so high-quality and very impressive. I noticed that the video came from a website named "Cancer Can Rock." Jay suggests that I get in touch with them. He informs me that this organization deals specifically with musicians who have cancer. This really piqued my interest, so I decided to reach out to them.

First, I went on their website. I saw that they had many videos of musicians recording in the studio. Many of the musicians were clearly very sick. I think to myself, as I watch one after another, what an unbelievable organization this is. I write down a name and a phone number off the website. I give the number a call and leave a message explaining who I am and what I do. The following day I receive a return phone call from the founder of Cancer Can Rock. The voice on the other end of the phone says, "Hello, I'm Jim Ebert from Cancer Can Rock. I went to your website and you look like someone we may be interested in." Then he says, "Let's talk about cancer first."

We share our stories with each other. I found out that he is a 17-year survivor of brain cancer. He is beating all the odds. He is someone I can look up too. He is strong and healthy and focused on what he is doing. He is out there helping people. I guess because people also helped him along the way. I think to myself: this is what I would like to do if I get through this alive. That is one of the reasons I decided to write this book. One of many reasons why I decided to write this book. As I sit here composing, I often think to myself: who am I to write a book? I never even read a book cover to cover (except for the Bible). Books are just not my thing, until now.

You see, cancer changes everything. There is a paradigm shift. There are actually some positive aspects to it, but you have to look for them. In my case, I feel I am now more aware about many things than I was before my diagnosis. I am more aware of others, and their feelings, and I am more aware of what they expect from me. I am aware of how fragile life is. If you are currently going through or have gone through cancer, or if you are currently going through treatments, or if you are going through any life-changing event, then you know what I am talking about. Life can turn on a dime. One minute you are healthy and doing your thing, the next minute, it can all be taken away, just like that. I am really aware of myself and who I am and what I am doing with my time. I am also a lot more optimistic now than I was before my diagnosis. You can ask anyone who has gone through it. We all belong to the same club and we are all connected. Those of us that have made it through are blessed and they are forever changed.

What can one say about Cancer Can Rock? It's a wonderful organization based out of Falls Church, Virginia. The founder, Jim, is a record producer from New York whose had several hit records and produced quite a few artists in pop music. He really knows what he is doing in the recording studio. Jim is a great guy and long-time cancer survivor. In our conversations, he told me, "You never really beat brain cancer. It never really goes away." My understanding is that it just lies dormant, and then one day when it decides not to be dormant anymore, it can become active again. That whole situation sounds pretty scary to me.

As scary as his story sounds, this is a great story with a great ending. Not that Jim has even come close to the end of his story.

Jim asks me to send him some music. I don't have a home studio or anything like that. I just use the voice memo app on my iPhone to capture any music ideas that I have. So, while I was sitting at home, I did start to write some songs. They were pretty dark sounding for obvious reasons. This was a pretty dark time in my life. I managed to put together about four songs to send him. It was just me, sitting in my living room with my acoustic guitar, singing and strumming. Believe me, these were pretty rough recordings. Much to my surprise, Jim liked this stuff! He liked one song in particular. You see, the deal is that they'll record you, but you have to have some kind of original song that is somehow related to your cancer or treatment or something like that. The song we recorded was, "It Don't Matter." It's a song about how I thought I needed all these things in life. Then all of a sudden, I was only interested in one thing, my health. All these things that I think or thought actually mattered, well, they don't. I have a whole new way of looking at the world now. If you have been diagnosed with cancer and go through chemo, radiation, or both of those treatments, or if you have had some kind of catastrophic event happen to you and you were lucky enough to come out on the other side of it ok, then you know what I am talking about.

It was now time to pick a date. Jim says he is available on August 14th. My final chemo was on

August 2nd. He asks if I'm sure I'm going to be all right by the 14th. "Oh yeah, man, I'm down; I'm in. Let's get those plane tickets." Oh man, was I wrong about that one. After each chemotherapy treatment, it took me longer and longer to recover. Looking back on it now, the truth is that I probably knew it was too soon for me to venture out, but I just could not wait to get back and become a functioning member of society again. I couldn't wait to return to the world. I wanted to have something to look forward to.

Well, needless to say – and unfortunately – I had to cancel because I was just way too sick. You see, my final chemo ended up being the one that really did me in afterward. I was sick for about three or four weeks. The chemo accumulates in your body so after your fifth or sixth session, you're really feeling it. I mean really, really feeling it. You don't want to move; you don't want to do anything. If you're lucky, you're running at maybe 65-70 percent of what your 100 percent should be. And that can go on for months.

I had to cancel that trip, and Jim gave me a new date weeks later. He even invited my wife to come along. So, we went together, and it was wonderful. Jim flew Karene and me up to Virginia, put us up in a great hotel, and provided Uber rides everywhere. Karene and I checked into the hotel. So far, it was just wonderful. A couple hours later, they picked us up and took us out to dinner.

Over dinner, we talked about music and life, cancer and conditions. We told each other stories; we talked about everything from guitars to movies to politics, and so on. I could tell right away that we were already becoming fast friends. It was a really nice evening all around. We were with Jim's friend and business partner, Rich Forsen. Rich is as cool as Jim.

Then we went over to the studio so I could check it out. There was a session going on. The guys there were kind enough to let us sit in the control room. We only stayed for a little while. We had to leave because it was getting a bit late and we had a 9:30 a.m. call time the following day.

They drop us back off at our hotel so we could get some sleep, and there are cars waiting for us again at 9 a.m. the following morning. We get in and drive over to the studio, I meet the recording engineer, and, one by one, the musicians start coming in. The guitarist shows up with all his gear, the drummer comes in, the bassist comes in. Jim is there too, and everything is going according to schedule.

So, we lined up some tracks and laid them down. Got some drum tracks first, and then built around those. Really organized, really professional musicians in a really professional studio. We recorded all day long, using some instruments I didn't think we'd be using, like a mandolin. We ended up taking the song in a whole new, different direction. It was a cool situation.

The last thing we recorded that day was the vocals. And let me tell you what – I was hurting. We'd been in the studio for about 12 hours at this point, and then it was time to do vocals! Surprisingly, it turned out that we got a really good track. And the whole thing was videotaped. So, I got a music video out of it, and a nice interview on YouTube. If you go to the Cancer Can Rock website, you can check out not only my stuff, but all the other artists as well. The day after Karene and I flew back home and we talked about what a great experience it was. We couldn't be more thankful.

After we leave, there are sound engineers doing all the mixing and mastering and the video guys doing all the editing and production of the songs and the videos. It costs thousands of dollars to complete the project, so if there's anything I can do to help, I'll always be on board.

A few months go by and I am starting to feel much better. I get a call from a local guy named County Mike. I don't know how he got his name. I guess he works for the county or something like that. Mike is a real nice guy, and he likes to run benefits with live music. He raises money for good causes and gives 100% of the proceeds to the charity that has been selected. He reached out to me and asked if I would be interested in doing a charity event where Cancer Can Rock would receive all the donations. I was more than happy to do so.

Mike was already hooked into this little club, Kelly Brothers Irish Pub in Fort Lauderdale. They have a lot of local blues artists who play there, and the pub is becoming a pretty important part of the live music scene down here in South Florida. We approach our good friend, Janice, who is the bartender/manager and go-to person at Kelly Brothers. If you want to get a gig, or if you want to get something done there, you've got to go through Janice. She agrees to host the event and putting it all together was intense. There were weeks and weeks of preparation. We got many local restaurants and clubs to donate. There were gift cards, raffles, 50/50s, and silent auctions. I called some friends who play in the music scene down here. We had about five or six bands come in and play for the benefit. Jim and his girlfriend Gina flew in from Virginia the day before the event. We hung out; they stayed at my house, and early the next morning we headed out to Kelly Brothers Irish Pub. The people came out in droves. It was a really wonderful outpouring of love and support, not only for me, but also for this charity that was doing things for both cancer patients and live music. We have a fabulous music community down here in South Florida, and I'm really proud to be part of it. We raised several thousand dollars for Cancer Can Rock that day. I'm so glad I was able to help make that happen.

The Cancer Can Rock organization is Jim's way of giving back. He decided to create this small company, and, being that he's in the music industry and unfortunately has been stricken with cancer, his way of giving back is by bringing in guys like me. There are many musicians who are going through cancer, and they may be going through treatments of some kind. Maybe they have finished their treatments. Regardless, bringing them into the studio to record for a day is an unbelievable gift. He records all types of musicians. Some are professionals, some are just locals in his neighborhood, you know, the local guys and girls who play in the restaurant or bar down the block. Jim creates precious memories for them and their families.

Some of these people have never even been in a recording studio before. Some of these people are like me, and they have never heard of Cancer Can Rock before. Because of Jim Ebert and Cancer Can Rock, these great folks get to experience what it is like to be in a professional recording environment, record a song with professional musicians, and have two videos posted on social media. All this is made possible by the enormous generosity of others.

Unfortunately, some of those folks that Jim records do not survive. But their families can now have this wonderful keepsake that will live on forever. There are interviews where the artists get to talk about the cancer and the struggles that they are going through. It's really just a wonderful experience. Jim is a giver; his mission in life is what he can give to others. It's not about making a hit record. It's not about making money. It's about what can he give to other folks who have been stricken by this disease. Personally, I believe that those who live a life by wondering, "What can I give?" rather than, "What can I get?" live a much richer, happier, and fuller life. The world is a better place because of people like Jim Ebert, Rich Forsen, and Cancer Can Rock!

Mom and Dad circa 1956

Mark and Donna 1963

1965

In this photo:
Guitar – Robert Allen Gibbs
Keyboards – Tom Regis
Drums - Fred Weng
Percussion – Rick (Rico) Geragi
Bass & Vocal – Mark Telesca

Photo by John Garbarino

Last show before starting chemotherapy

Hematology and Oncology Center Lantana, FL

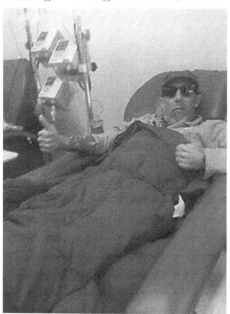

A visit from blues musician Rockin' Jake

Selfie during chemo in between treatments

First show back after treatments
Two Left Feet Blues Festival
Simsbury, CT

Cue Recording Studios Falls Church, VA for Cancer Can Rock

Jim Ebert

Record Producer
Founder of Cancer Can Rock
Cancer survivor

Fur Peace Ranch

With one of my heroes, Jorma Kaukonen, signing my beloved Martin 000-28

Gigging in Boca Raton, FL

LOVE MUSIC HATE CANCER

Proud to be endorsed by Delaney Guitars

Photos by Jay Skolnick

Back at the Funky Biscuit

Karene, Mariah, and me circa 1999

Here we are again

August 3, 2019

8

LET'S GET REAL

In this chapter, I would like to talk about a number of different things. Things that I believe to be serious. Especially when it comes to beating cancer. Things like faith, procrastination, journaling, fear, visualization, exercise, diet, and the will to do something.

Faith is something that got me through all of the operations, the cancer and the chemotherapy treatments. I had faith in my doctors, and I have faith in others. I even have faith in myself. I have faith that there is some type of higher power. I am not particularly religious, at least not in an "organized religion" sense, and I don't know what that higher power is, but I have faith that there is something supernatural going on, and it's good. Here is something else I believe to be true. Having faith in something that you can see, feel, and touch is really no faith at all. Faith is what you have when you are looking forward to having something work out for you. For instance, I have faith that people are going to read this book. I don't know if they will, but I have faith that they will. I believe they will. That is why I am putting the better part of two years into writing it.

As we all move forward in life, we don't really know if all the dots are going to connect. You just have to believe they are going to connect, and if they don't, just look at it like it's another bump in the road, and that maybe you haven't got the right perspective just yet to see the connection. In my opinion, that is what faith is.

So, if you have cancer or some other illness, or if you are going through some difficulties in life, please believe you are going to get through it, get healthy, and remain healthy. Hey, it's worth a shot. It will put you in a better frame of mind for when some additional difficulties enter your life. Personally, being positive and having the faith that things are going to fall into place really helps me focus on certain things in my own life.

I used to play all these different mind games with myself. I used to make up all kinds of crazy scenarios in my head. "What if this happens?" or "What if that happens?" That kind of thinking is all rubbish. In my opinion, you are better off if you live in the present, and create your future, and do your best not to become a victim of the circumstances that you created for yourself.

Procrastination is the intentional action of delaying or postponing something. I've struggled with procrastination all my life.

I'm pretty sure that procrastination is something all of us have had to deal with from time to time. Some have it worse than others. I think it's a disease, and everyone I know is infected – it's gone viral! Ever since getting diagnosed with cancer and realizing the uncertainty of life, I now consciously try to focus on the things I used to let slide. Things that I would do halfway and then give up on. There are lots of projects that I had left undone. In my opinion, procrastination should be qualified as a legitimate disease. So many people have it; so many put off until tomorrow what they can do today. What's the old joke? – "People say I procrastinate too much, but be patient, I'm thinking about working on it soon."

Like I said, I'm so guilty of this, but I'm trying really hard to change that. I'm just grounded a little bit better now. I'm more self-aware, believing in myself more, and doing what I really believe I'm here to do. I feel like procrastination can cripple you. I feel like it has crippled me in the past. The truth is this, I had set a specific date on when I wanted this book to be completed. That specific date came and went! So, here I am, still writing, it's many months later and I'm still working on it. What happened? One day goes by, then another day goes by, and another, and then I realize that four days have passed, and I haven't done anything to advance its completion. Then I start to feel pretty bad about it. I start to feel bad about myself. I have to ask myself, "Am I losing interest in this?" I truly do believe in this book. I believe that it will help at least a few people if not many. It is that belief, the belief that I am doing something to help others, that keeps me moving forward toward completion. Here is another way of saying it. I have the faith that this book will help someone who is, or who has gone through, the same or similar struggles as me. There is the answer I was looking for. Believing that I can help others is giving me that motivation. It is giving me the will to keep my eye on completion. My belief and my faith in myself, and this book, is overcoming the feelings of procrastination that, like a thief in the night, can rob you of your sense of purpose and achievement.

Another way I try to overcome procrastinating is by trying not to do too many things at once. I don't know about you, but for me, daily living eats up a lot of time. Between working, taking care of the house, laundry, shopping, taking care of my mother-in-law, taking care of the dogs, and trying to make sure that my adult daughter stays on the right track at all times, my hands (and days) are pretty full. Plus I still need to find time for paying the bills, going out with my wife for some down-time, going to blues festivals and participating in some of them, keeping my band busy, keeping my calendar full with good-paying gigs, and writing new songs. This is all very time consuming. Then I try to add on writing a book, making new CDs, helping out friends and family, and the list goes on and on. It doesn't make me special or anything like that. I am sure that many of you are in the same situation. Life moves so fast these days. I even find it hard to find the time to quiet my mind! Even if it is only for a few minutes.

Sometimes I feel like I don't have enough tentacles to properly control everything that I have going on. I often get myself into a situation where life can become overwhelming. So lately, I am truly consciously trying to do less. I've come to the realization that you can't say yes to everything and everyone. These days, I pick and I choose what I am going to do, and just do a better job at what I choose to do.

I feel like it is a much healthier way to live. So slow down if you can. I know we all move at a different pace. Please try to be aware of your most inner feelings, and you will know for yourself if you are doing too much.

Will. The will to live. Will is a higher faculty. I believe that when you have the will to do something, and when the will to do it is the motivating force, then you are living on a higher vibration. If you focus on the will to do something, it seems to quiet everything else. It seems like you only have one thing on your mind. That's very important, especially since keeping a positive attitude is essential when it comes to getting healthy. I know that for me, it always seems like I am thinking of multiple things at the same time.

To truly focus on something, it needs to be practiced. It's not something that you can do once or twice. Keeping one thought in your mind, and one thought only for an extended period of time, is something I find difficult to do. It's easy when you're young. When I was four years old and playing with my toy soldiers, hours would pass without interruption. It gets harder as you get older to find and keep that kind of intense focus, particularly when you are alone. If you are currently in chemotherapy or something equivalent, then you are probably spending a good amount of time at home. I am sure that you are alone with your thoughts quite often. So, find the will to focus intensely like you did when you were a kid and accomplish things! The first thing on the list should be to get healthy and in shape. Second on the list is to stay healthy and in shape. Third on the list is to repeat the first two things. You'll be glad you did.

While we're on the subject, let's talk about **staying fit and staying in shape**. Now I know that exercise and diet can be a real struggle for many people. There are many, many problems in the United States as far as our food supply is concerned. While I was home during my chemo treatments, I was watching a lot of Netflix documentaries on health and food. It was very eye-opening for me. I needed to figure out if there is anything I can personally do to help prevent cancer from ever coming back.

So, I wondered, what can I do to help myself get fit? I found that I really had to look on the inside to figure it out. I always heard a lot of people say, "You have to look within." I never really gave it too much thought. But when I got sick, a lot of things came into play for me. I was forced to think about a lot of things I had never thought of before.

Here is what I came up with regarding getting in shape and staying in shape. You know that having a positive attitude is the key to all this stuff. I am not going to go into any discussion on what having a positive attitude is. You all know what it is. There are only two types of attitudes as far as I'm concerned – a good positive attitude and a bad, shitty attitude. There is nothing in-between.

First, if I'm going to get in shape, I need to keep it simple, very simple. With everything that I have going on in my life just being a regular American, I do my best to keep things simple. Here is how I look at it.

We live in two different worlds, right? Our inside world and our outside world. I had recently become aware of a theory, or thought process, or whatever you might like to call it. It's pretty easy to notice that many, many people are more concerned with their outside world than their inside world. In this day and age of Facebook, Instagram, Twitter and whatever other social media sites we all travel to, it's no surprise that we are all becoming more concerned about what's going on with our friends and our community and our "outside world" than we are about ourselves and our "inside world." I notice that many of the millennial generation are addicted to social media. With all this constant information coming into our lives, it gets harder and harder to pull away from our phones and computers. But getting in shape and staying fit requires that we make time for our inside selves.

I'm just saying that everything I do needs to be efficient and organized. Having realized this, if my inside world is not organized, then my outside world will not be organized. Another way of saying this is if you are organized inside your head, then you will be organized outside of your head. There are a million different ways to say this. It's getting the concept of it. That is what matters here.

So, the first thing I needed to do was make time to collect, and to keep, the thoughts in my head organized. I needed to spend more time alone living in my "inside world" and organizing things.

I just want to be fit and stay fit with the least amount of physical effort as possible. So, in order to accomplish this, I needed to get my head together first.

I'm not the kind of guy to get an expensive gym membership and buy new shorts and sneakers to go lift 20-pound dumbbells in public. Who am I kidding? I'm not even going to make it to the parking lot of the gym.

When it comes to exercise, here is my deal. I started doing push-ups. That's it! I certainly would not consider myself a physically strong person. When I started doing push-ups, I am embarrassed to say, I could only do about one or maybe two. The chemo treatments had really taken a major toll on my body. I was so weak; I just couldn't stand it. So, in order for me to get stronger, I would just drop to the floor whenever I got inspired to do so. I just started doing them, and after the first week, I was doing five in a row, then six, then seven. I am currently up to about 15 now. For me to do 15 push-ups, it takes me about 20 seconds. So, I do 13 to 15 push-ups whenever I feel like it. Sometimes two or three times a day. My workout takes between 40 and 70 seconds per day.

So maybe doing pushups isn't your thing. Then just

make it a simple exercise that is right for you. Maybe it's just something as simple as bending over and touching your toes or stretching. The thing is this, when it comes to diet and excrcise, you have to do *something* about it. Especially as we get older or are just coming out of some type of treatment. It'll make you feel better and stronger. You can get very good results by working out 40 seconds a day!

Diet. The reality is that I had to do something about my diet. Who knew how unhealthy I was eating? I spent years in bars eating hamburgers and fries. I was drinking sodas and sports drinks and eating fast food. I was eating all kinds of bad food, and I was eating too much of it. I spent more than 50 years eating poorly. Essentially my body was a dumpster and I didn't even realize it. In my defense, it was the way I was brought up. I was just eating all the same stuff I was eating all my life, until I started watching those Netflix documentaries. I couldn't stop watching them, and I couldn't believe our government's involvement in our food supply, not to mention how American farmers are being treated.

So, here is what I decided to do for myself. First, you know for me, it has to be simple. So, I decided to cut my sugar intake by about 80%. I stopped drinking sweet drinks like soda, sweetened iced tea, lemonade, sports drinks, energy drinks, and any and all drinks that contain artificial sweeteners. I also cut way down on white bread and white potatoes. I eat whole wheat bread instead now. I started cooking and eating more fish. I also bought a juicer and a Nutribullet. I juice veggies around once a month.

When I eat and drink during the day, I think about what I am eating and drinking. I go to my "inside world" for one second and decide if the food I am about to eat is good for me or not. Now for me, it took some practice to think about that. I can't tell you how many times I would be halfway through a meal and then realize, I shouldn't be eating this! It's those little things that make big changes.

At night now, I may have some ice cream or even some chocolate so I can get my sugar fix. I know this is not great for me, but I am aware that I didn't have any sugary foods during the day. So, I'm okay with it.

Pretty much the only fast food I eat now is a veggie sub on whole wheat bread from Subway. I'm not a big fan of cold cuts anyway.

So, this is the lifestyle change that I made as far as my food intake goes. I use almond milk in my coffee now. It has some sugar in it, but it's not tablespoons of sugar.

This simple change in diet has kept weight off. I weigh 25lbs. less than I did before my cancer diagnosis. I weigh myself every day, sometimes twice a day. I really should be between 160 and 165 pounds. I am now living between 165 and 170 pounds. Nobody's perfect. If I see myself getting near 170 pounds, I just go get a $5 veggie sub. The next day, I'm back to 166 or 167 pounds. Also, I now no longer have to take any medications for acid reflux, high cholesterol, or high blood pressure.

I believe our bodies are a miracle and a gift and need to be taken care of. That's all I'm going to say about getting into shape and getting healthy.

Fear is a pretty strong word. Fear, like procrastination, can cripple you. It can be a major obstacle in your life if you are trying to accomplish something. There is an element of fear in all aspects of life. I know a lot of people who have a fear of dying. That is understandable, fear of the unknown. I totally get it. There are many people who have the fear of success. This is also fear of the unknown. Some folks are just so used to not achieving any real significant levels of success that they are actually afraid of it. So, if you are trying to overcome something like cancer, you just have to be aware that perhaps you may also have to overcome your fear of success.

How one would work on overcoming the fear of success is something that I really do not think I am qualified to discuss. I have no formal training in any of these areas. I am just sharing with you my thoughts, opinions, and experiences. If you feel you have issues that are centered around fear, then perhaps you should seek out some professional counseling. It's available everywhere these days, and it's also covered under many insurance plans.

Another thing I started doing during my recovery is **journaling**. Journaling looks like it's going to be a significant part of my life. It's not a diary of what I did on a particular day. Rather, it's a guide of how I want to see my life unfold. I am writing a script for my life on how I would like it to turn out. Simply said, I write down my hopes and dreams in my journal. We all have hopes and dreams. For me, writing it down and reading it back makes me look at life a bit differently. I worry more about what I am putting out, rather than taking in. There are a lot of folks worried about what they can get. I used to feel like I didn't get enough respect, or I didn't get enough love, or I didn't get that promotion at work, or I don't have enough money. After my diagnosis, and while in recovery, I just decided to write down in my journal what I could give. I started asking myself, "What can I do to give back to my community?" Everyone, whether they know it or not, is involved in some type of community, whether it be large or small. I'm in the blues community. This community rallied behind me while I was fighting for my life. Writing this book is just one way of giving back. The more you give, the more you get, regardless of the situation. It brings you back to the faith aspect of life. So, write down your thoughts and ideas and hopes and dreams. Read them back to yourself. Hopefully you will find the motivation and the will to do something for others. You will be rewarded in return. The great news is that hopes and dreams and ideas are all free!

Visualization. Having cancer, and not knowing if the treatment is going to work, makes me think of life this way – I came up to the edge of a cliff. What I mean by the cliff is that I was facing the possibility of actually dying. Let's start over. I came to the edge of the cliff, I looked over, and then I stepped back. I visualized myself stepping back, and I kept stepping back away from the cliff. It was an exercise in visualization. I did it pretty often. It was something that I practiced. It felt funny at first, but it quickly became a part of my routine and I truly believed it helped me. I honestly believe that my visualization of stepping back from the edge of the cliff formed an unconscious internal process that helped my body to step back and heal. I also learned something there on the edge of that cliff. After coming so close to death, the other side isn't something to be feared. It was almost kind of peaceful in a way. It was the acceptance of it. Very strange feeling indeed, and it really was just crossing over. I didn't feel like my mind was going to die, just my body. I used to be afraid of dying, not so much anymore. I think that the visualization exercise had helped me overcome that fear. When I was going through cancer and treatment, even if I was thinking of something else or doing something else, there was this underlying current of how sick I was, and it never seemed to escape me. This, I now believe, is perfectly normal. I am over two years in remission, and that underlying current is still there, and it is strong. You're so aware of what you've gone through. The further away you get from the experience, I think the better you understand it.

Now, I know that this is going to sound hard to believe, but there have been many positive outcomes in my post-cancer life. One of the most positive outcomes is within my marriage. My wife Karene and I have always been really close, but I think we're even closer now. You know, the thought of me actually dying and no longer being around sent shock waves through her system. It's something that was so real – that dying was a possible outcome. There is now a new sense of appreciation that I think my wife has, not just for me, but for life in general. I also have a new sense of appreciation for everything that I encounter in life, particularly the things we encounter together.

I used to sometimes get caught up in things and get high-strung about things. The bills are coming in and I'm wondering if there is enough money coming in to pay on time. Doctor bills and insurance, and things like that. I just don't do it anymore. You truly can worry yourself to death over money.

Now we both seem to pay less attention to those things. We're still very much aware of what our financial responsibilities are, but we don't freak out about it. So, if I have a bad week, a slow week with a couple of days off, a couple of low paying gigs, I think about the great week I'll have coming up, even if it's a month or two away. That'll make up for it. I have faith that all the dots are going to connect. So, there's a lot more peace in life.

Another positive outcome is that things seem to have slowed down quite a bit for me. I'm moving at a slower pace. Not because I'm getting older, but because I'm choosing to move at a slower pace. I was always that guy who had a lot of oars in the water. I always had more stuff going on than I was able to handle. Now I have fewer things that are outstanding, and I'm completing more things.

Tasks are getting completed, and it's a wonderful feeling. I also realize that I am very fortunate that I am able to play music for a living. I used to work a day job, and it took all day! Funny how that works! I would then come home and answer emails, pay the bills, eat dinner, clean up after dinner, rush to a gig, and have very little time for me. By choosing to live at a slower pace, I have more time now for what really matters in my life. It's very important. I'm not going to let myself go crazy any longer. It's a simple decision. You can make that decision for yourself right now. It takes no effort and no money to make the decision, but you will have to practice it. You must practice slowing down. I know it sounds crazy, but you'll get a lot more done!

There is one more thing that I had started after chemotherapy and it may sound strange, but I feel like it really helped me. Every day I take a cold shower for 60 seconds, then I turn on the hot water. I do it because it's uncomfortable. That is the point of it. So, as I go through my day and my life, I occasionally find myself in an uncomfortable situation or position. I think about the cold shower and how I handle that. It just helps me deal with the situation at hand. It also helps build my self-confidence. You should try it.

9

NOW WHAT?

Now what? That is the big question. What do I do now that I have been given a second chance at life? If I really think about what I just said, it's pretty heavy. I know I'm one of the lucky ones. How come I made it? How come there are so many that don't make it? I don't know; it's a mystery. I realize there are many people who don't get a second chance. If you are reading this book, perhaps you are one of the lucky ones too.

If so, you may notice that many things have changed for you. You can choose to approach your diagnosis in one of two ways. You can find the positives in all of this, and yes, it is very possible to find something positive in something that seems so negative, or you can take a negative approach. That's all there is. There is no middle ground here; there is no other way. You can either be positive and live your life, move forward, accomplish things, have achievements, be fulfilled with happy and healthy relationships – or you can dwell on the negative and say things to yourself like, "Why me? Things never go right for me. Things will never be the same again." Well, maybe that last part is true. But maybe things can get better. I know they did for me.

I just do things from a different perspective these days. I try to take each moment and get the most out of it because you never know how much longer you're going to be here, or when your last minute is going to be lived. So, it's kind of a scary thing. One day you're on top of the world. You have everything, you're moving forward, and then, bam. It can be all over in a couple ticks of the clock, and without you even realizing it.

So, I will tell you about some more changes that I have made in my life. These are things I never would have even thought about had I not been diagnosed with cancer.

In an odd kind of way, I found something positive in a negative experience.

I know I've written about being "positive" and being a "positive person" in this book. But how do you become a positive person? Here is what I came up with that works for me. Being positive and optimistic is something we need to train ourselves to do. At least that seems true for me.

For me, being positive all boils down to one word: habit. As humans, we are all creatures of habit. Most of us have good habits. Nearly all of us have some bad habits (at least one). Regardless, we all have habits. The thing I continue to try to do is realize which habits are good for me and which are bad. Very simple stuff here. If you have a bad habit of stopping at fast food restaurants every day, try eating at home before you leave the house instead. If you can do that for one week, you are on your way to living a healthier life. Say you only do it for a day or two. Okay, that's fine, it was your first try. Try it again in a couple of days. Go shopping at the market instead or check out some YouTube videos. Find the inspiration. I find inspiration sometimes by seeking out inspiring videos. They are informative, and the right ones can be very helpful. This is one way I become inspired. Another thing I do is form new habits. Of course, these days, I only form habits that are beneficial to me and my life. I am an ex-smoker; 17 years now without a cigarette. That was a real bad habit for obvious reasons. Like many, I found it very difficult to quit. Somehow, I found the courage to quit smoking. Ever since then, I am very careful about which habits I pick up.

I spoke earlier about taking a cold shower each day for 60 seconds. If I miss a day, do you know what I do the following day to make up for it? I take a 60 second cold shower and I choose not to beat myself up for the day I missed. I stopped being so hard on myself. Taking a 60 second cold shower each day has become a habit for me. I don't have to do anything to motivate myself to do this. If I don't do it for several days, I really start to feel bad about myself. I know that when I do take the cold shower, it improves my day and energizes me. I am aware that the shower is only one aspect of my life that makes me feel a little better about myself, if nothing else. I do the same with push-ups. Every day I do a good number of push-ups, just because it makes me feel better. It also makes me physically stronger. More positive vibes coming my way. My mind thinks about it, my body follows, and the spirit to do more push-ups just appears like magic. It gets me ready to take on the challenges of a new day. It gets me ready to take on some risks.

Sometimes taking the right risks is really what life is all about. Everything that we do takes on an element of risk. It's a risky world that we live in. Getting married is a risk, having kids is a risk, getting that new job is a risk, buying a new car is a risk, driving that new car is a risk. Changing the way we see ourselves is also a risk. Changing the mindset of where we fit in while living in this world is a risk. Taking on a new belief system is a risk.

Here is something more to think about. Becoming more self-confident is a risk, believing in yourself is a risk, and getting others to believe in you and what you are doing is a big risk. Investing the money you saved is a risk.

You can help yourself work your way back to good health. Ask any cancer doctor. The first thing they will tell you is that you must have a strong, positive outlook on your treatment and life in general. They all say it because it is true. You just have to believe you are going to make it through. However, like most things in life, it's certainly easier said than done. Saying we believe something, and truly internalizing it and making it part of our inner being, making it part of the fabric of our lives, is not always easy. However, it truly is attainable. Perhaps it is through the practice of meditation for some. For others, it may be something different.

If you are having trouble finding the motivation for yourself, perhaps you could look into joining some support groups. There are cancer support groups everywhere. Every hospital and every school should have some type of support group. I have not done a whole lot of research on this, but I am sure there is a group for everything.

Here is another crazy habit that I have formed after my diagnosis with cancer. I bought myself a red-light bulb. I have a space in my house where I go to work on me. Every time I walk into the room, I turn on the red light. The red light, for me, means it's time to get serious. This is the place where I work on me. When that light is on, I am doing my job. I am doing tasks big and small. I could just be writing in my journal or doing some push-ups. Or thinking of new ways I can accomplish something, or sending out emails, or maybe I am just meditating. This is all me working on me, and I am enjoying it. This is my red-light habit. I am building a stronger relationship with myself.

Think about what I just said: building a stronger relationship with myself. We all spend so much time worrying about the relationships we have going on in the outside world that we sometimes neglect the relationship we should be having with ourselves.

Everything changes when you get a cancer diagnosis. All relationships change, especially the one you have with yourself. Your whole outlook on life changes.

There are so many profound things that happened for me when my outlook changed. One is that I feel more grounded. Once I was on the other side of my treatment, and it looked like it was going to work, I instantly felt like a more solid and grounded human being.

So here I am, telling you about my life and my journey through cancer. I'm telling you how much has changed for me since my diagnosis. I want you to know how I have really gotten "in tune" with myself and my surroundings. I want you to know how much more aware I am of my own mortality, not the mortality of dying, but the mortality of being truly alive.

You and I know that this life is going to end for us all. No one knows when, or how, but we all know it's coming. I seriously thought it was all over for me. Like I said before, I know that I am one of the lucky ones, so if you are one of the lucky ones like me, you have to ask yourself, "What do I do now? Now that I have a second chance?" Or maybe a third or fourth chance for some of us. I know that for me, I have made a very conscious decision to turn the most horrible thing that ever happened to me into the most positive thing that ever happened to me.

I am a survivor!

EPILOGUE

I know that I'm lucky. I am now in a group of people who have survived cancer. We all share our stories. We have to. It's important to each and every one of us.

I hope my story can be at least somewhat inspiring to you. I know everyone's journey through cancer is different. Perhaps after reading about my journey through cancer, we can find some common ground.

I am not a psychologist or a psychiatrist or any type of mental health professional. I have no training on any of the subjects I have discussed in this book. This book is just my journey through cancer, chemotherapy, and recovery. I'm just a regular guy who happens to play blues music for a living. This book is my way of explaining to you what I did to get better and what benefitted me the most. In a short story called "Sonny's Blues," James Baldwin says, "For, while the tale of how we suffer, and how we are delighted, and how we may triumph is never new, it always must be heard. There isn't any other tale to tell, it's the only light we've got in all this darkness" (p. 47). I hope my tale can bring a little light to you in your time of darkness.

APPENDIX

In this section of the book I have compiled a small list of organizations that are willing to help musicians and other entertainers that have been stricken with cancer and other life changing events. They are in no particular order and please be aware that each organization will have its own criteria for eligibility. Again, this is just a small list of resources that will help you get started should you need any assistance.

THE HART FUND
℅ THE BLUES FOUNDATION
421 S. Main
Memphis, TN 38103-4440
PH: 901-527-2583
Website: blues.org

HEALTHCARE BLUEBOOK
5880 Nolensville Pike
Suite 200

Nashville, TN 37211
Website: healthcarebluebook.com

HEALTHWELL FOUNDATION
P.O. Box 489
Buckeyestown, MD 21717
PH: 800-675-8416
Email: grants@healthwellfoundation.org
Website: healthwellfoundation.org

JAZZ FOUNDATION OF AMERICA
247 W. 37th Street
Suite 201
New York, NY 10018
PH: 212-245-3999
Email: info@jazzfoundation.org
Website: jazzfoundation.org

MUSICARES
11 West 42nd Street, 27th Floor
New York, NY 10036
Phone: 212.245.7840
Fax: 212.245.8130
Toll-Free Help Line: 1(877) 303-6962
PH: 212-245-7840
Website: grammy.com

ACTORS FUND
729 Seventh Avenue, 10th Floor
New York, NY 10019
PH: 212.221.7300 ext. 119
Fax: 212.764.6404
website: actorsfund.org

BROADCASTERS FOUNDATION OF AMERICA
125 W. 55th Street 4th Floor
New York, NY 10019
PH: 212-373-8250
Email: info@thebfoa.org
Website: http://www.musiciansfoundation.org

GOSPEL MUSIC TRUST FUND
P.O. Box 932
Brentwood, TN 37024
PH: 615-969-2781
Website: gospelmusictrustfund.org

HEALTH ALLIANCE FOR AUSTIN MUSICIANS
3010 S. Lamar Blvd
Suite 200
Austin, TX 78704
PH: 512-541-4226
Email: info@myhaam.org
Website: myhaam.org

MUSICIANS FOUNDATION
875 Sixth Avenue
Suite 2303
New York, NY 10001
PH: 212-239-9137
Email: info@musiciansfoundation.org
Website: http://www.musiciansfoundation.org

MUSIC MAKER RELIEF FOUNDATION
224 West Corbin Street
Hillsborough, NC 27278

PH: 919-643-2456
Email: 411@musicmaker.org
Website: musicmaker.org

NEW ORLEANS MUSICIANS' CLINIC
1525 Louisiana Avenue
New Orleans, LA 70115
PH: 504-415-3514
Email: info@neworleansmusiciansclinic.org
Website: neworleansmusiciansclinic.org

PINETOP ASSISTANCE LEAGUE
P.O. Box 1916
Clarksdale, MS 38614
Email: pinetopperkinsfoundation@gmail.com
Website: pinetopperkinsfoundation.org

THE HAVEN FOUNDATION
PH: (615)200- 6896
http://www.thehavenfdn.org

MUSIC HEALTH ALLIANCE
2021 Richard Jones Road, Suite 160
Nashville, TN 37215
PH: 615-200-6896
Fax: 1-800-934-1977
Email: info@musichealthalliance.com
website: www.musichealthalliance.com

SWEET RELIEF MUSICIANS FUND
2601 E. Chapman Ave., Suite 204
Fullerton, CA 92831
PH: (714) 626-0447
Email: info@sweetrelief.org

website: www.sweetrelief.org

MARK TELESCA
https://www.marktelesca.com

MARK TELESCA FACEBOOK
https://www.facebook.com/marktelesca

MARK TELESCA INSTAGRAM
https://www.instagram.com/marktelesca/

BLUES FOUNDATION
https://blues.org/

BRI BLUES RADIO INTERNATIONAL
http://www.bluesradiointernational.net

CANCER CAN ROCK
https://cancercanrock.org

THE FUNKY BISCUIT
https://www.funkybiscuit.com

JAY SKOLNICK PHOTOGRAPHY
https://www.jskolnick.com

SOUTH FLORIDA BLUES SOCIETY
https://www.soflablues.org

SOUTH FLORIDA'S MUSIC MAGAZINE
https://www.sflmusic.com

DATFLYS CONCERT VIDEOS
http://www.youtube.com/datflys

DELANEY GUITARS
https://www.delaneyguitars.com

Baldwin, James. "Sonny's Blues." *The Jazz Fiction Anthology*, Ed. Sascha Feinstein and David Rife, Bloomington: Indiana UP, 2009, pp. 17-48.

THANK YOU

You know who you are....

SHARE YOUR STORY
BEGIN YOUR HEALING PROCESS HERE

In this last section, I offer you the opportunity to try journaling and visualization. This is your chance to write out your frustrations, your pain, your hopes, and your dreams.

_____
_____
_____
_____
_____
_____
_____
_____
_____

LOVE MUSIC HATE CANCER

LOVE MUSIC HATE CANCER

LOVE MUSIC HATE CANCER

LOVE MUSIC HATE CANCER

LOVE MUSIC HATE CANCER

LOVE MUSIC HATE CANCER

LOVE MUSIC HATE CANCER

LOVE MUSIC HATE CANCER

LOVE MUSIC HATE CANCER

AN EXERCISE IN VISUALIZATION
By Usui Reiki Master Jessica Delgadillo

What is visualization?

Visualization is a technique of focusing your creation energy into a desired outcome – it is a way of directing your focus and making the choices you want to make. Rather than allowing yourself to think like a victim of circumstances, visualization helps you to choose what you want. It is important to note that each person has a unique way of processing so the image you visualize might be clearer or more vivid for some than others, but no one way is better than any other. It does not matter if the image is clear or blurry. The important part of visualization is the focus and intent.

How do I do it?

Visualizations almost always begin with a breathing or relaxation exercise followed by conjuring a mental image on which to focus your thoughts and energy.

Let's try a breathing exercise to get you started.

Inhale slowly counting to 8 (or choose a number that feels comfortable to you). Exhale slowly counting to 8. Inhale counting to 8. Exhale counting to 8. Inhale counting to 8. Exhale counting to 8. Continue until you feel the rhythm of your breathing and your body relax.

Continue to breathe deeply. Now imagine that you see a bubble form in front of you. See the bubble as it forms. Now feel the fear and anxiety inside you. See the fear take form and push that form into the bubble. Imagine the fear leaving you and filling the bubble in front of you. When you're ready, take the bubble in your hands and blow it away as you exhale. Watch as it floats away from you. Further and further it flies until it is merely a dot on the horizon and disappears. Once you can no longer see the bubble, imagine that space inside you where the fear once was fill up with a golden light. As you focus on the light imagine its warmth spreading through you, enveloping you. All you feel while wrapped in this light is health and peace. Repeat this exercise as needed.

LOVE MUSIC HATE CANCER

LOVE MUSIC HATE CANCER

LOVE MUSIC HATE CANCER

Made in the USA
Columbia, SC
14 January 2020